MW01253252

Sam Mihara's
FLY FISHING ALASKA©

A Guide to Enjoying Alaska's Waters and Saving Money

By SAM K. MIHARA

ESKAY PUBLISHING CO.
HUNTINGTON BEACH, CALIFORNIA 92649

Sam Mihara's
FLY FISHING ALASKA ©; A Guide to Enjoying
Alaska's Waters and Saving Money

ISBN: 0-9656258-0-X

Published by:
Eskay Publishing Co.
16821 Greenview Lane
Huntington Beach, California 92649

*Cover photograph of John De Arment on the
Talachulitna River by Sam Mihara*

CONTENTS

CONTENTS (CONTINUED)

Acknowledgments

Special thanks:

My appreciation goes to many who helped in making this book possible, including:

Vicki Hogue for editing

Moira C. Harris for design and layout

Sharon Vlchek for photo scanning assistance

Dee Thomas for helping coach me in my seminars

Paul Cyr and Mack Minard from the Alaska Department of Fish and Game for advising me on preferred rivers and species of fish.

Preface

PREFACE

I have been to Alaska for fly fishing every summer for the last 10 years. I have also been to many other parts of the world including Argentina and New Zealand seeking the best of angling. I have seen firsthand the many interesting problems faced by fly fishing travelers to the dreamland for fly fishers.

A typical problem is disappointment in the quality of fishing for the amount of money spent. Where to go, when to go, what equipment to take and how to save money at the same time are typical issues that have come up.

I also learned how to solve such problems. From this experience, I developed a seminar on planning an affordable, high quality fly fishing experience. That seminar has been provided to many fly fishers throughout the U.S.

Satisfaction surveys of my seminar audiences indicated strong satisfaction with my fly tying demonstrations and slide shows. But many suggested I write a book on the topic. They especially wanted more useful information on planning the ideal visit to remote locations for quality fly fishing at low cost.

This first book resulted and contains the major lessons I learned over the years on how anyone can plan for and enjoy a better fly fishing experience at an affordable cost.

WARNING—DISCLAIMER

The purpose of this book is to provide information on fly fishing in distant locales.

It should be understood by the reader that the publisher and author are not professionals in the travel, economics, financing, transportation, accounting, outdoor safety and survival, wild animal handling, entomology and emergency medical services professions. If such specialty expertise is needed, the reader should seek the services of competent professionals in the business.

The purpose of this book is to inform the reader based on the experiences of the author. It is not the objective to copy all the information available from other resources. But it is the goal to provide summary information from several sources believed to be accurate and informative. Please refer to all available information and tailor the information to your needs.

Although efforts have been made to accurately state actual experiences and references and report on other sources of information believed to be accurate, there may be mistakes in this book, either by omission or by error. This book is, therefore, intended to be a general guide and not the ultimate or final authority of information up to the date of this publication.

The intent of this document is to entertain and provide general educational guideline information. The publisher and author shall have neither the responsibility nor liability to any entity or person with respect to any loss or damage caused, or alleged to be caused, directly or indirectly by the information contained in this book.

If you do not wish to be bound by this Warning-Disclaimer statement, you may return this book to the publisher for a full refund.

Chapter

1

WHY FLY FISH IN ALASKA?

A fly fishing seminar was given by Curt Gowdy, the noted sports newscaster and fly fisherman. Someone asked him, "You have been all over the world. If you had to pick the best location for fly fishing, where would you go?" Curt hesitated for a moment, then responded, "Alaska, for its variety, abundance and opportunities to improve my personal fly fishing skills with big fish."

In addition to Curt Gowdy's reasons for going to Alaska, there is another good reason to go: Alaska is an important salmon fishing region within the United States. Because of the abundance of salmon, you can bring home your catch and not have to pass customs inspection. This is not true about international destinations. Fresh fish from other countries cannot be imported into the United States without proper licenses. So, for people who want to bring home a large quantity of fresh salmon, Alaska offers many rivers for meeting that objective.

Many of the rivers in Alaska are easily wadable or reachable by boat. If you get to your well-planned destination at the right time, the odds for very high quality fly fishing are good.

There are few other spots in the world where you can experience five species of salmon spawning and providing food for many species of native fish, including large rainbow trout, colorful char and spirited arctic grayling. All of these species congregating in one river provides the chance to catch a wide variety of fish without traveling long distances.

Fly fishing in Alaska also affords many opportunities to take excellent photographs. The daylight hours during summer are long, and the beauty of the water and surrounding terrain set a perfect background for photos of large fish caught on flies.

With all that Alaska has to offer, you want to be sure your trip is problem-free. That's why I find it amazing to see so many people go to such a faraway place without making adequate preparations. They go to great expense and take the wrong equipment, take too much equipment, or go with unrealistic expectations, and, consequently, return disappointed.

I have seen many unhappy visitors to Alaska:

> ❖ At Anchorage International Airport in mid-summer, I saw travelers who went into a panic when they arrived at the rental car counter with no reservations and were told the rental car agency had rented all of its cars. The traveler sent his family scurrying to other rental counters only to be given the same answer by all the rental agencies. Their trip was ruined before it began.

> ❖ I went on a fly fishing trip on the Kenai River where a fly fisherman from Florida brought a

new lightweight, $1,000 rod and reel combination onboard the boat. He was told by the guide, politely but firmly, "Sorry, we don't allow that gear when I guide." The Floridian was furious.

❖ I know of several fly fishers who have gone to the famous Kenai River on their first visit to Alaska. To their disappointment, they discovered large numbers of densely packed fisherpeople near the premium intersection of the Russian River and the Kenai, standing elbow to elbow, casting for the same fish.

❖ There was an outstanding, skilled fly fisherman who went to Alaska for the first time, wanting to sight fish, and discovered that the Kenai River was a glacial melt river. It was milky, opaque and impossible to sight fish. Disappointed, he returned to California.

❖ I met a fly fisherman who paid for an expensive lodge trip expecting that everyone on the trip was going to fly fish. His main objective was to fly fish for king salmon. But to his disappointment, he was assigned to a team where the other members used only conventional spinning gear. He wrote letters of complaint to the lodge owner because he wasn't able to achieve his main objective, to fly fish for king salmon, but to no avail; the season for kings had already ended for the year.

❖ When I land at Anchorage, it amuses me to see

many fisherpeople bring large plastic carrying cases for their fishing rods. These cases are typically the homemade variety that are about 6 inches in diameter, 6 feet in length, and made of PVC piping purchased from the local hardware store. I have seen an airport baggage handler throw these fly rod cases on the concrete floor like stacks of cordwood.

❖ It is common for many lodges to promote their rivers as excellent sources of king salmon fishing in mid-summer. And frequently the king salmon fishing is as good as advertised. But sometimes rivers are closed to king salmon fishing for conservation reasons. And guests may not be told of the local prohibition on king salmon fishing until after they arrive at the lodge.

❖ On one of my trips, I was drifting slowly downriver, when I came across a couple who were huddled near a tree, shaking. When I asked if they needed help, they said they had just had a surprise encounter with a bear and did not know how to cope with the problem.

❖ Then there was the time I wanted to get closer to the fish-holding portion of a stream. It required my getting slightly over waist high in water. I misjudged the drop-off of the river and the loose gravel started to give way. My neoprene waders were cinched at the waist with a belt and air was trapped in the waders below the waist. As I slipped into the water, my head sank below water level because of the heavy weight of the gear in my vest. Fortunately, I am a fairly competent swimmer and was able to compensate for my sinking upper body. But I had not anticipated the buoyancy problem.

Almost everybody I have briefed at my seminars feels there must be a better way to enjoy Alaskan fly fishing at lower cost, or to get more value for the money paid, or to reduce the risks of fishing in the wilderness. Therefore, this book is dedicated to those who want to avoid problems and seek high quality fly fishing in Alaska at a minimum of expense.

Chapter

2

TODAY'S DILEMMA—
HOW TO PLAN AN AFFORDABLE TRIP

When I give my seminars, I frequently ask how many people in the audience have been to Alaska? Usually, about 80 percent have not. When I ask why they haven't been, the answer is sometimes not knowing where and when to go, but for most people, the answer is affordability.

A common perception of the cost of an Alaskan trip is that such a desirable fishing visit will cost upwards of $5,000 or

more, plus airfare, for a week. This is above an affordable and reasonable budget for many fly fishers, although it may be affordable to someone who has saved enough money to put into a trip of a lifetime and wants to be certain that the trip will be an outstanding and memorable experience. This is why I have included lodges that are expensive, but well worth the quality of fishing, accommodations and special services provided.

Most people, though, want to find a more affordable venture for a week of fly fishing, so I have included trips that cost under $1,000 per week. To plan the trip that is right for you, use the following process to narrow down the alternatives that make sense for you.

THE PROCESS

All processes have a beginning and an end. To plan the ideal fly fishing trip, you begin by deciding on your objective.

Is your objective to combine a week of sightseeing and fishing? Or is it to find premium fishing for the duration of your visit? Do you want to go for a single specie, such as the biggest king salmon or the heaviest rainbow trout possible? Are you interested in acrobatic somersaulting fish like silver salmon? Or maybe the chum salmon that plays tug-of-war with the fly fisher is more to your liking? Or are you going for multiple species at the same time? You must first identify your objective, before you can proceed and develop a desirable plan.

The next step is to decide what you can afford. Planning an overall budget that you cannot exceed is important if, like most of us, you have practical budget limits.

Completing these first two steps, defining your objective and deciding on a budget, will help you choose your desired species, and when and where to go for those species.

Saving on travel and lodging are major concerns to long-distance fly fishers. Saving on travel involves searching for group fares and package lodging arrangements. There are many types of lodging available, varying from very high-quality, full-service lodges to austere do-it-yourself cabins with commensurate prices.

Identifying the minimum equipment needed to take on a trip helps save money. And planning a minimum number of flies to take is important for the budget-minded. Finally, learning to pack luggage for the air trip to avoid extra baggage costs will further lower your overall expenses.

The final step is to put your trip plan in writing. Make a checklist of the things you need to do to plan your trip. This list might include identifying prices, location, time period, transportation, equipment and what to pack.

Now that you understand the basic process, you can proceed to develop your plan.

Chapter

3

THE PLANNING STAGE
THE FIRST QUESTION—WHAT IS YOUR OBJECTIVE?

In this chapter you will:

❖ Decide on your objective for your Alaskan trip.

❖ Learn how to develop your trip plan based on this objective.

Let's be realistic, when you plan a major fishing trip, do you first consider your objective? If you're like most people, you probably select your destination, pick your lodging and buy your equipment before considering what you are really looking to get out of your fly fishing trip.

Clarifying your objective is the most important step to take before planning a trip anywhere, and it applies even more so to fly fishing in Alaska. The reason it is so important to clarify your objective before planning your Alaskan trip is because of the abundance of species and rivers in Alaska. Randomly selecting a location before considering the species desired may result in disappointment. The type of fish desired for fly fishing may not match the selected river, or the time of year selected may be poor for the heaviest concentration of that fish. A heavy concentration of fish is desirable for effective fly fishing.

As variety, abundance and skills improvement are important to Curt Gowdy on his Alaskan fly fishing trips, your objectives may be different. Is the challenge of finding and catching a record size of a given specie more important than variety? You may wish to target selected rivers where records for biggest fish have already been set. Or you may want abundant variety in the same week at the same location.

COMBINING SIGHTSEEING WITH FISHING

If this is your first trip to Alaska, you might wish to combine sightseeing with fishing, especially if you go with a spouse who doesn't share your devotion to fly fishing. If combining sightseeing and fly fishing is your objective, staying close to a central city like Anchorage may work best for you, especially if you have only a few days to spend on your trip. For the uninformed, it is difficult to find a lodge that allows guests to stay only a few days. Most lodges accommodate guests for at least one week at a time. Similarly, float trips average a full week in duration and the scenery, although many are on scenic rivers, is limited. Some exceptions for brief stays are given in this book.

Here are some suggestions for a combination trip:

✦ Use Anchorage as your base and go sight-seeing in Denali, Kenai, Valdez and surrounding glaciers and parks. Then combine sightseeing with fishing in one-, two- or three-day trips to the Kenai or Talachulitna rivers or to private cabins, using daily fly-outs from Anchorage. (See Chapter 13 and Appendices 2 and 3 for day trips.)

✦ Rent a car and drive along the major highways to the north, east and south, stopping to do some local stream fishing. During the peak salmon runs, you should expect large numbers of people who do the same thing, though, and

you may find the favored spots overcrowded. Maps of highways and local streams can be ordered from sources contained in Appendix 2.

✦ If you are in Anchorage on business or as a central base for your vacation and are interested in a day or two of uncrowded fishing, you can fly out from Anchorage's Lake Hood or Merrill Field to remote, privately owned or government owned cabins (Appendix 3).

Next, decide what species of fish you would like to catch. The two classes of fish that are abundant in Alaska are the natives (trout, char and grayling) and the five species of salmon that come up Alaskan rivers from the Pacific Ocean to spawn. Different species, sizes, equipment and locations are described in Chapters 4 and 5 and Appendices 1 and 2.

DEDICATED FLY FISHING

For those of you who wish to pursue fly fishing exclusively while in Alaska, a popular objective is to catch the maximum number of different species within a short time. For example, my personal record is seven species in one week, but I keep trying for eight species or more (five salmon, rainbow, char, grayling). This objective sets the best time of year as typically mid-summer. For my objective, the best odds exist by going in late July and counting on a late run of king salmon and early run of silver salmon.

The best location for obtaining all species in a week is the

Bristol Bay drainage, but other rivers in the south central region have record size fish and need to be considered for a single species record.

If you wish to focus on a particular type of fish, Chapter 5 will help identify the best time to go for each fish species.

Here are some other possible objectives:

> ✦ For 40-pound and above king salmon, try the Bristol Bay region. This region has a strong run of kings beginning in late May to early July. They stop at convenient places to rest where deep holes and relatively calm waters exist. The best technique for catching them is to use attractive flies and heavy sink tips to get to the bottom of the holes. For proper equipment for catching kings, see Chapter 4 on equipment and Chapter

6 and Appendix 1 on the best flies to take.

✦ Sockeye salmon is a favorite of those who seek high quality and flavorful fish. They are elusive because they are not feeding and are dedicated to spawning in rivers, so using special flies that attract the sockeyes during their migration is the key. They arrive in mid-June through late July in many rivers in the southwest region. But the peak of the season is in early July.

✦ If your objective is a tough fighter like the strong chum salmon—the sensation is like hooking onto a runaway freight train—all of July and most of August is generally good.

✦ Pink salmon have a strange behavior: Most pinks arrive to spawn in even years (1996, 1998, 2000). No one knows what clock mechanism the pinks have that tells them it's an even year. But they arrive in abundance beginning in late July and continuing through early August, and are found concentrated shoulder-to-shoulder near mouths of rivers, not going too far upstream to spawn.

✦ The goal of catching acrobatic silver salmon can be a good one during late summer—coincident with the rainbow run in August and September.

✦ For enormous rainbows, over 24 inches and 6 pounds (they grow very heavy from feeding on salmon eggs all summer), the late run in September and October is best. Early summer in June can also be good for catching the hungry trout that wait for the salmon to arrive and lay eggs.

✦ Other native fish, such as large arctic grayling and arctic char, are fishable during the same time as the rainbow, so you can plan on going for rainbow and get these other premium Alaskan fish at the same time.

The actual time of expected arrival of salmon may vary depending on the specific location. Even if you can pinpoint a week of arrival, the time might be early or late by several weeks. During early planning, you should talk with the lodge or guide of your choice on the expected timing of the fish you desire and the desired flies. Then talk again a few weeks just before the trip to see if the timing or the flies have changed.

GUIDED VERSUS SELF-GUIDED

In Alaska, I have been to populated, well-trekked areas for fishing, as well as to remote interior locations in the back country where I saw few, if any, other people.

As a result, I have developed a simple rule on whether or not to use a guide: If you are traveling to waters that you know are frequently visited and you have access to emergency assistance, no guide is needed. But if you are entering into an unfamiliar, remote location with inexperienced people, use a guide.

Most of Alaska is too remote to do experimenting on your own. To cope with hazards and assure safety, have an experienced, able guide ready to help at any time. You made too much of an investment in travel and time to not consider using a guide when entering an unfamiliar, risk-laden environment.

If you are on a restricted budget, consider using a guide for a short trip to gain experience. Then a return visit without a guide may be acceptable if you have the necessary skills to assure a safe trip.

DEFINE YOUR OBJECTIVES AND CREATE AN OVERALL PLAN

Once you have picked your desired fish species and time of year to go, you must reserve early. Reserving one year ahead or earlier is not too soon. The reason is that the seasoned fly fishers know the best times at the best rivers and reserve annually to return. So the only way to get in on the best timing is to do it early.

If your goal is to sight fish, many rivers are created from opaque runoffs of glaciers and are a milky turquoise color, making sight fishing impossible. But some of these rivers, like the opaque Kenai, have set all-time records for sizable fish. The Kenai holds the Alaskan record for river-caught salmon at 97 pounds for a king salmon.

So start your plan with a good definition of your objectives, which in turn will help clarify the best location, preferred time of year and expected water conditions. And above all, define your objectives and plans early; a year ahead of a trip is not too soon. Chapters 4, 5, 7, 8, 9 and 13, and Appendices 2 and 3, will help you create your optimum plan.

SOME QUICK ANSWERS

If you want to find some satisfying trips without going through a systematic process, go directly to Appendix 4 and review the seven recommended locations and lodging. These vary in price from high to almost no cost, and I have personally had satisfying experiences with all seven.

Chapter

4

FISH SPECIES, RIVERS AND EQUIPMENT TO MATCH

Now that you have defined your objective, the next steps in planning are to:

✧ Consider the various species of fish available.

✧ Find out the best time of year for catching the species in which you are interested.

✧ Make a list of the rivers where you can find your desired species.

This chapter gives general guidelines to fish species, matching equipment to species and names of primary rivers where you can find your desired species. Not all species available in Alaska are listed, but those most commonly sought by fly fishers are referenced. Not all regions in Alaska are included, but the waters that most appeal to fly fishing enthusiasts for sight fishing with flies are rivers and streams in the Southcentral region (north, east and south from Anchorage) and the Southwest region (rivers in the Bristol Bay and Kuskokwim Bay drainages). The Southeast region has excellent fishing, but inclement weather is more likely here. Readers who have additional views on other regions are invited to write to the publisher.

To further develop your plan, see Chapter 5 for details on the premier rivers to visit and information on lodging and float trips for those rivers. Appendices 2 and 3 give more lodging details and discuss transportation.

ARCTIC GRAYLING

These colorful grayling with large dorsal fins are very interesting, mainly because they are the one fish that can be easily seen, are not afraid of people, are not leader shy and are ready and eager to devour both floating and wet flies. Watching a grayling holding in a clear pool and rising up to 6 feet or more to a dry Humpy or Caddis is pure entertainment. The same

grayling will aggressively take a Hare's Ear or AP Black nymph. Even walking in a gravel bed causes live nymphs to be kicked up and you can see grayling coming to your feet as you walk.

Grayling are light, averaging 1 to 2.5 pounds. A trophy is considered to be 4 pounds. The record for Alaska is 4 pounds, 13 ounces, caught in 1981 in the Ugashik Narrows. Grayling may be caught throughout the open water season (May to October).

Grayling can be caught with a wide range of light to medium rods, anywhere from weight numbers 2 through 7. If your goal is to use a single rod for multiple species, including salmon, a number 7 will work fine. But if your goal is to catch native fish in the spring or late fall, then a lighter rod should suffice. A floating line is fine with quick changing, medium-sink-rate sink tips or using sinkers on the tippet. Leaders should be 2- to 4-pound test.

Although there are grayling found in many lakes, I find the challenge of sight fishing in clear rivers and creeks a very satisfying experience. There are many desirable clear rivers and creeks for arctic grayling, but a selected list for sight fishing grayling in moving water includes the following:

Southcentral (Anchorage) Region
Gulkana River, northeast of Anchorage
Talachulitna River, north of Anchorage
Talkeetna River, north of Anchorage
Ugashik River, north of Anchorage
Upper Susitna River, north of Anchorage

Southwest (Bristol Bay Drainage and Kuskokwim Bay) Region
Alagnak River, flowing out of Nonvianuk Lake
Aniak River, near Aniak
Goodnews River, west of Dillingham

Kanektok River, south of Bethel
Kvichak River, flowing out of Iliamna Lake
Togiak River, west of Dillingham
Ugashik Narrows, west of Anchorage
Upper Nushagak River, north of Dillingham

CHUM SALMON

The chum salmon is, in my opinion, one of the strongest fighting fish in Alaska, next to the king salmon. When a chum take a fly, it feels like hooking on to a runaway freight train, making it essential to have a reel with a good drag system. Or you may wear gloves to apply hand braking to the rim of the reel, but watch out for the fast spinning reel handle.

I know a surgeon who damaged his operating fingers when a runaway salmon was hooked. This is one reason that right-handed people should learn to use left-handed winding for reels, in case of such high-speed runs by large fish. Another alternative is to use anti-reverse reels, but the extra cost may

not be worth it for fly fishers who rarely go for big fish.

Chums arrive in rivers from mid-June through mid-August. The typical weight is between 6 and 12 pounds. A trophy is 18 pounds. The record is 32 pounds, caught in 1985 at Caamam Point.

Equipment for chums should include a 9 foot, number 6 through 8 weight rod, although an 11 will do fine. An 11 rod is appropriate if you are catching king salmon as well as chums.

The lines should be wet lines only, with extra fast or Type III shooting taper sink tips. Chums rarely strike surface flies, since they cruise at middle and lower levels of water. Leaders should be 6- to 10-pound test.

These rivers are excellent for fly fishing for chums:

Southcentral
American and Dog Salmon Rivers, Kodiak Island
Chuitna River, on Kenai Peninsula
Talachulitna River, north of Anchorage
Talkeetna River, north of Anchorage
Willow and Little Willow Creeks, north of Anchorage

Southwest
Alagnak River, flowing out of Nonvianuk Lake
Aniak River, near Aniak
Goodnews River, west of Dillingham
Kanektok River, south of Bethel
Kvichak River, flowing out of Iliamna Lake
Nushagak River, near Dillingham
Togiak River, west of Dillingham

Dolly Varden or Arctic Char

It is difficult to differentiate between dolly varden and arctic char in the field. They both have a dominant skin pattern, and attractive light purple spots on the body, like their close relative, the eastern brook trout. These fish, collectively called chars, are available all year and arrive in the rivers following the salmon coming to spawn. The average weighs between 1.5 to 4 pounds. A trophy is 8 pounds. The record for Alaska is 19 pounds, 12.5 ounces, caught in 1991 in the Noatak River.

Suggested equipment for char is a 9-foot, number 4 through 7 rod. Lines can be both floating and sink tip, or floating with sinkers on the tippet. Char rarely rise, but can be seen aggressively chasing simulated eggs or salmon flesh following spawning.

Excellent rivers for char are found throughout Alaska anywhere that salmon have heavy runs, but outstanding rivers include the following:

Southcentral
- Copper River System, northeast of Valdez
- Kasilof River, in Kenai Peninsula
- Kenai River, in Kenai Peninsula
- Little Susitna River, north of Anchorage
- Russian River, in Kenai Peninsula
- Talkeetna River, north of Anchorage

Southwest
- Alagnak River, flowing out of Nonvianuk Lake
- Aniak River, near Aniak
- Goodnews River, West of Dillingham
- Iliamna River, near Iliamna Lake
- Kvichak River, flowing out of Iliamna Lake
- Newhalen River, flowing into Iliamna Lake
- Togiak River, west of Dillingham
- Upper Nushagak River, north of Dillingham
- Wood River lake system, west of Anchorage

KING SALMON (AKA CHINOOK, TYEE, SPRINGER OR SPRING)

The mighty king is the premier large salmon for Alaska. For many fly fishers to Alaska, catching at least one king on a fly is a personal triumph and a sought after goal.

It takes work and conditioning to pursue kings, because heavy equipment is needed for these large fish. Heavy sink tips are essential to get to kings that cruise near the bottoms of rivers and recover in deep holes on their way to spawning. In some locations, it is possible to sight kings upstream closer to the spawning areas in shallower waters, but they will not be as fresh as those in the tidewater or estuary areas near the mouths of rivers.

Kings arrive in many rivers from around late June through late July. However, check with your selected guide or lodge to confirm the most likely dates for kings on that river. As usual, do not accept a date not within the likely "window" of best opportunity for kings. It will be near impossible to catch kings on a fly at less than peak times. Spend the time to search for alternate rivers if a guide or lodge is not available at the preferred time. The best planning solution, however, is to plan early and book early with a firm date at the peak times.

The average king weighs about 35 pounds. A trophy is a huge 50 pounds and is a real test for rods. The record king for Alaska is 97 pounds, 4 ounces and was caught on the Kenai river in 1985.

Rods should be 9 feet long and in the class of number 10 through 12 weights, with an 11 being optimum. Lines should be sink tips, because kings will not surface. Sink tips must be high density to reach the bottom of rivers and holes when working the deeper tidal or estuary waters. Also essential is adequate backing, at least 150 yards and 30 pounds. Leaders should be 12- to 20- pound test with a minimum of 200 yards of 20-pound backing.

The largest freshwater kings in Alaska have been taken in the Southcentral region. However, the Southwestern region has very high quality and abundant numbers of kings—some rivers have averaged 20 kings per boat of two or three fly fishers, which is a very high rate of catches. Excellent rivers for kings include:

Southcentral
Anchor River, on Kenai Peninsula
Karluk and Red Rivers, Kodiak Island
Kenai River (Alaska record, 97 pounds), on Kenai Peninsula
Kasilof River, on Kenai Peninsula
Moose River, on Kenai Peninsula
Susitna River (feeder streams), north of Anchorage
Talachulitna River, north of Anchorage
Talkeetna River, north of Anchorage

Southwest
Alagnak River, Bristol Bay, flowing out of Nonvianuk Lake
Aniak River, near Aniak
Goodnews River, west of Dillingham
Kanektok River, south of Bethel

Naknek River, Bristol Bay, flowing out of Naknek Lake
Nushagak River, near Dillingham
Togiak River, west of Dillingham

PINK SALMON (AKA HUMPY OR HUMPBACK SALMON)

Pinks arrive in late July through late August. The strange characteristic of pinks is that they primarily come up rivers during the even numbered years: 1996, 1998, 2000, et cetera. No one knows what clock mechanism pinks have that tells them which year is even.

The average pink weighs about 3 to 5 pounds. A trophy is 8 pounds or above. The state record for pinks is 12 pounds, 9 ounces. This record pink was caught in 1974 in the Moose River, which flows into the Kenai River.

Equipment for pinks should include rods in sizes 6 through 8 weight. Lines should be both floating and sink tip. Flies used for chums and kings are effective for pinks.

Rivers for pinks are throughout Alaska, mainly near the mouths and tidal waters. Excellent rivers for pinks include:

Southcentral
Bird Creek, 45 minutes south of Anchorage
Kamishak River, southwest of Anchorage
Kenai River, on Kenai Peninsula
Kodiak rivers near outlets, Kodiak Island
Little Susitna River, north of Anchorage
Lower Kenai River, on Kenai Peninsula
Talachulitna River, north of Anchorage
Talkeetna River, north of Anchorage
Willow Creek and Little Willow Creek, north of Anchorage

Southwest
Goodnews River, west of Dillingham
Kanektok River, south of Bethel
Kvichak River, flowing out of Iliamna Lake
Nushagak River System, near Dillingham
Togiak River, west of Dillingham

SILVER SALMON (AKA COHO SALMON)

Silver Salmon are the last to arrive in Alaskan rivers, typically between early August and mid-September. They average between 8 to 12 pounds. A trophy silver is 18 pounds or more. The record size silver for Alaska is 26 pounds, caught in 1976 in the Icy Straits.

Silvers can be caught with rods in the 6 to 8 weight class. The lines used should be wet lines only, with extra fast or Type

III shooting taper sink tips. Silvers rarely strike surface flies, but they cruise at middle and lower levels of water. Leaders should be 6- through 10-pound test.

Excellent rivers for silver salmon include the following:

Southcentral

Bird Creek, 45 minutes south of Anchorage
Kamishak River, southwest of Anchorage
Kasilof River, on Kenai Peninsula
Kenai River, on Kenai Peninsula
Little Susitna River, north of Anchorage
Moose River, on Kenai Peninsula
Russian River, on Kenai Peninsula
Talachulitna River, north of Anchorage
Talkeetna River, north of Anchorage
Red Salmon or Allgaions River, east of Cordova
Wasilla Creek, north of Anchorage

Southwest

Alagnak River, Bristol Bay, flowing out of Iliamna Lake

Aniak River, near Aniak

Goodnews River, west of Dillingham

Kanektok River, south of Bethel

Naknek River, Bristol Bay, flowing out of Naknek Lake

Nushagak River, near Dillingham

Togiak River, west of Dillingham

Ugashik River, on North Alaska Peninsula

SOCKEYE SALMON (AKA RED, KOKANEE OR BLUEBACK SALMON)

Many consider the sockeye salmon, or red salmon, the premier eating fish in the salmon family. Fresh sockeye caught and quickly cooked with a marinade or plain with simple seasonings is a real treat when fly fishing in Alaska. Sockeyes arrive in early July through mid-August. They average between 5.5 and 8 pounds. A trophy is considered to be 12 pounds or heavier. The record is 16 pounds, caught in 1974 in the Kenai River.

The preferred equipment for sockeyes is a number 6 through 8 rod. Lines can be floating with sink tips or sinkers on tippet or weighted flies. None of the salmon are leader shy and using a 15-pound leader without a tippet is common and effective. The sockeye fly is unusual in that the best flies are tied very sparsely, a few wraps of bright hackle near the eye is all that it takes. (See section on the ten flies to take.)

Southcentral

Kamishak River, south of Anchorage

Kasilof River, on Kenai Peninsula
Kenai River, on Kenai Peninsula
Little Susitna River, north of Anchorage
Moose River, on Kenai Peninsula
Russian River, on Kenai Peninsula
Talachulitna River, north of Anchorage
Talkeetna River, north of Anchorage
Wasilla Creek, north of Anchorage

Southwest

Alagnak River, Bristol Bay, flowing out of Iliamna Lake
Goodnews River, west of Dillingham
Kanektok River, south of Bethel
Nushagak River, near Dillingham
Togiak River, west of Dillingham
Ugashik River, on North Alaska Peninsula

WHERE TO STAY—ALASKA'S PREMIER RIVERS AND LODGING

Next, follow these steps to decide where to stay:

❖ For each river on your list, look at Appendix 2 for lodging and prices.

❖ Prepare a list of lodges, camps and floats in your price range.

❖ Narrow your list down to a single choice based upon price and availability.

With so many waters to choose from, which river should you target? Now that you have pinned down your desired species and the general waters where you can find those species, your next step is to narrow down your choice of rivers. The following are significant premier rivers from Cook Inlet to Bristol Bay to Kuskokwim Bay drainage, from east to west.

Be sure to ask questions of representatives of each lodge or guide service to get more information on the likely fishing prospects and timing of your visit. Don't make up your mind on a single selection until you have the facts about each river and lodge for the time you want to go.

AMERICAN CREEK

Located in Katmai National Park about one hour southwest of Anchorage. Access is by commercial airline to the town of King Salmon, then local air taxi to Katmai National Park. An alternative is to take a float plane from one of several fly-out lodges into one of the lakes that is on the American Creek.

The water is very clear here, resembling many picturesque streams and small rivers in the lower 48 states. It is easy to sight fish for rainbows and chars. American Creek has many tributaries, and can be floated with an experienced guide. Also,

there are many bears in this area and ample opportunities for taking close-up photographs of them (see Chapter 15 on bears).

Rainbows, char, grayling and sockeyes are abundant here. Char are almost "one on every cast" during salmon spawning.

The rainbows are attracted to all classic trout flies, especially Cream Elk Hair Caddis, Parachute Adams and Sam's Ugly Numbers 1 and 2 (see Chapter 6 to determine which flies to take). Use artificial lures, and catch-and-release fishing, which are required. The best time to go is in early summer and late summer/early fall.

There is no permanent lodging on American Creek. Adjacent lodging and other services include:

➥ Angler's Alibi. Full-service tent camp; optional fly-outs; moderate prices. (See Appendix 4.)

➥ Campgrounds at Katmai National Parks. Low prices.

➥ Grosvenor Lodge. Full-service lodge within Katmai Park; moderate prices.

➥ No See Um Lodge. Full-service luxury lodge; daily fly-outs; expensive.

➥ Katmailand, Inc. Guide service; cabins or tents; float trips; low prices.

➥ Ouzel Expeditions. Guided floatfishing with tents.

➥ Branch River Air Service. Air taxi.

See Appendix 2 for more information on lodging, prices, and current fishing quality, and reservation information on low-cost cabins. Also, contact local guides for up-to-date information on prospects in the region. See Appendix 3 for air taxi service to the rivers.

ALAGNAK RIVER

This river is one hour southwest of Anchorage. Fly into King Salmon, then take a floatplane to the spot of your choice along the river. There are several lodges and float concessions available for lodging (Appendix 2). Alagnak is not accessible by car.

The Alagnak is very good for fly fishing—rated as one of the five best rivers in Alaska. The water is clear, and the river has a gravel bottom. But use caution, the river is fast in certain areas, and it is difficult to find crossing spots. There are many bears, moose and caribou along the river, especially during the salmon run (see Chapter 15 for a discussion of bears). The river's whitewater is mostly Class I with some Class II.

King salmon are abundant in this river and of excellent quality in the lower river. The run peaks during July. My personal record size for king salmon was 55 pounds caught on the Alagnak. Chum, sockeye and silver salmon are also very good here. Pinks are mainly in the even years. The number of trout and grayling are fair in the Braids section of the upper Alagnak river. The Department of Fish and Game is currently doing research into the reason for the drop in rainbows.

Use artificial lures only, a single hook per line, and no bait. (Chapter 6 lists the 10 best flies to take and Appendix 1 gives a more complete listing of recommended flies.)

There are many lodges on the Alagnak, and many outboard fishing boats in the lower river during king salmon season. The upper river is a good location for low-cost float camping, but fishing for king salmon is difficult from floats.

Lodging on the Alagnak includes:

➡ Alagnak Lodge. Full service; no fly-outs; moderate prices.

➡ Angler's Alibi Tent Camp. Full service; some fly-outs; moderate prices (see Appendix 4 for specific recommendations).

➡ Branch River Lodge. Full service; no fly-outs; moderate prices.

➡ Cabins at Nonvianuk Lake. Very low cost.

➡ Katmai Lodge. Full service; optional fly-outs; moderate to expensive.

ANCHOR CREEK

Anchor Creek is located on the Kenai Peninsula, about four hours drive from Anchorage and about one hour north of

Homer. Or fly to Homer or Kenai and rent a car.

The water is clear except following rains. The fishing is excellent for both salmon and halibut in nearby Cook Inlet waters.

Anchor Creek is excellent for catching king salmon in early summer, rainbow and dolly varden in late summer and autumn, silver salmon in late summer and pink salmon in even years. This river is famous for excellent steelhead trout in September and early October. Be ready for crowds because of easy road access.

Lodging and guide services include:

→ Anchor River Inn. Full-service lodge; guides available.

ANIAK RIVER

This river is on the Kuskokwim river system. It is about one hour from Anchorage by air to Aniak village. This area is not accessible by car.

The Upper Aniak is clear, with water coming from other lakes and streams. Logjams could make floating difficult. There are many snags in deep pools in the middle of the river. The scenery is beautiful and there are many wild animals, including bears, moose and caribou.

This river is very good for fly fishing rainbow trout, char, grayling, and king, silver, pink and chum salmon. Upstream, use only unbaited artificial lures and catch-and-release for rainbows.

Lodging and services in this area include:

→ Alaska Dream Lodge. Full-service lodge with guides; daily fly-outs; moderate to expensive.

→ Aniak River Lodge. New full-service lodge with guides; low prices (see Appendix 4).

→ Eruk's Wilderness Tours. Floatfishing.

→ Ouzel Expeditions. Floatfishing.

BIRD CREEK

Located 30 minutes by car south of Anchorage. This is an easy drive with convenient access to the river. It can be very crowded in the summer because of the salmon runs and the close proximity to Anchorage. This area is a nice diversion for people with several hours to spare in the city.

Contact the local Department of Fish and Game for rules and regulations at (907) 267-2218.

The water here is generally clear except during heavy rains. There are sockeyes in mid-summer. The silver salmon run begins in late summer and lasts through October. There are some pinks in even years, and chums and char.

There is no permanent lodging on Bird Creek, but there is

plenty of lodging available in Anchorage. There are also campgrounds nearby.

BROOKS RIVER

This river is located in Katmai National Park about one hour southwest of Anchorage. Take a commercial airline to King Salmon, then local air taxi to Katmai National Park. An alternative is to take a float plane from one of the several fly-out lodges to Brooks, or stay in King Salmon and take a boat to Brooks.

This river has very clear water with many tributaries. It is famous for rainbow trout and sockeye salmon. There are many bears in this area, and many opportunities for taking close-up photographs of them (see Chapter 15 on bears).

The fish are abundant in the Brooks river. They include rainbow trout, char, grayling, chum salmon and sockeye salmon. Use artificial lures only. For catching rainbows, Cream Elk Hair Caddis, Parachute Adams and Sam's Ugly Numbers 1 and 2 are very effective; for catching sockeyes, use Sockeye Orange fly (see Chapter 6 on the ten flies to take). Catch-and-release fishing only. The best time for fishing is early summer and late summer/early fall.

Lodging and services include:

➡ Brooks Lodge. Large facility in Katmai National Park.

➡ Campgrounds in Katmai National Park

➡ Kulik Lodge. Full-service lodge with daily fly-outs; moderate to expensive.

➡ Ouzel Expeditions. Guided floatfishing.

CAMPBELL CREEK

Campbell Creek is located in Anchorage. By car, go to Dimond Boulevard. You can fish up to the Department of Fish and Game marker at the C Street bridge. Because this area is within the city, it is very crowded during silver salmon season from July 25 to October 1. But fishing here is still a nice, low-cost diversion for people who are in the city and have a few hours to spare.

The water is generally clear except during heavy rains. There is accessible fishing on both sides of the creek. Contact the local Department of Fish and Game office at (907) 267-2218 for the latest rules.

There are many places to stay in Anchorage. Some lodging facilities are only a short walk to Campbell Creek.

CHUITNA RIVER

This river is located on the west side of Cook Inlet, just west of Anchorage. Take an air taxi or helicopter to Chuitna River from Anchorage airport. There is no modern road access, but primitive gravel roads exist in the area.

The water in this river is clear, and there are several tributaries. There is very good fishing for king salmon in early summer, silver salmon in late summer, and pink salmon in mid-July during even years. You can access the middle and upper river by the gravel road for good rainbow and dolly fishing. Or take a helicopter to the upper river and raft down to the mouth for pickup.

Lodging and services include:

➟ Alaska Helicopters. Helicopter taxi.

➟ Chuitna River Guides. Float trips.

➟ Ketchum Air Service. Air taxi; cabins.

COPPER RIVER (SOUTHWEST)

The Copper River flows into Lake Iliamna, about 45 minutes by air west of Anchorage. It is not accessible by car. Several lodges service this area. Be aware that there are two Copper Rivers. The one we are discussing here is a clear-water river in the Southwest district, not the major glacial river near Cordova.

The water in this river originates from nearby lakes. It is famous for its rainbow trout, and is easy to float and fly fish in. A waterfall is located about 12 miles upstream from Lake Iliamna that is a barrier for most fish.

The sockeyes are outstanding, though relatively mature by the time they arrive in the Copper. The river also boasts excellent large rainbows, char and grayling that feed on salmon eggs. The Copper is good for dry flies and egg patterns during spawning. Only fly fishing is allowed in most parts of the river, and catch-and-release on rainbows.

Lodging and services include:

➡ Iliamna Air Taxi. Float trips.

➡ Rainbow King Lodge. Outstanding, large, full-service luxury lodge; daily fly-outs; expensive (see Appendix 4).

➡ Rainbow River Lodge. On Copper River; no fly-outs; limited to local waters.

DREAM CREEK

Located on Gibraltar River, which flows into Lake Iliamna, Dream Creek is one hour west of Anchorage. Take a commercial airline into the town of Iliamna. Stay at a local lodge or obtain guide service at Iliamna.

Dream Creek offers outstanding opportunities for catch-and-release of large rainbows from summer through fall, with larger fish in the fall. Sockeye salmon are abundant in mid-summer.

Wind can be a hazard for floatplanes, so flyers may require access to Kakhonak airport and strip for wheeled airplanes.

There are no permanent accommodations on the river or creeks. The following list shows services available in the town of Iliamna.

➡ Iliamna Air Taxi. Air taxi

➡ Rainbow King Lodge. Full-service luxury lodge; daily fly-outs; expensive.

GOODNEWS RIVER

The Goodnews flows into lower Kuskokwim Bay. It is about one hour from Anchorage by jet to Dillingham or Bethel. Take a floatplane to Goodnews. There is no road access.

This river has beautiful scenery and is very popular for fly-in fishing in July and August. Be prepared for bad weather in the lower river; good quality rain gear is essential.

The Goodnews River is very productive and mainly known for float fishing. It has very clear water. Take a floatplane into the lakes and lower river. You can expect enormous runs of all five species of salmon, very good char, dolly varden and grayling, and large rainbows.

In the Togiak National Wildlife Refuge area, only artificial lures are allowed.

There are no permanent lodges on the river. Spike camps and guided float fishing are available.

The following lodging and transportation can be found in this area:

➡ Alaska River Safaris. Spike camp.

➡ Freshwater Adventures, Inc. Floatplanes.

➡ Kuskokwim Aviation. Wheelplanes.

➡ Ultimate Rivers. Guided float fishing.

GULKANA RIVER SYSTEM AND COPPER RIVER (SOUTHEAST)

This area is easily accessed by car because the Gulkana river runs along the Richardson Highway. Remote sections are accessible by floatplane. Boats and rafts can be put in at various points.

Clear water drains into this river from many lakes and streams, but it can be clouded by heavy rains. The main Copper River is silt-laden and opaque from melting glaciers.

The king salmon are very good here in early summer. Grayling fishing is very good all summer and fall. There are sockeyes from mid to late summer and rainbow trout from late summer to early fall.

The following lodging and services are available:

⇾ Alaska Wilderness Outfitting Company. Float trips.

⇾ Gulkana Air Service. Air taxi.

⇾ Lee's Air Taxi Service. Air taxi.

⇾ Paxson Lodge. Full-service lodge.

⇾ Ruffitters. Float trips.

KAMISHAK RIVER

This river is 200 miles southwest of Anchorage. Take a float-plane from lodging in Iliamna or wheelplane and land on the beach at outlet of river. Not accessible by car.

This area is very scenic for its winding river and the adjacent snow covered high mountains: Mount Douglas and Mount Augustine.

Outstanding chums inhabit the river in July, chars from July through September, pinks in August, and silvers from September through October. The upper river is an excellent place to sight fly fish for chars. My personal record for char was a 26-inch 6-pound fish from the Kamishak River, using Sam's Ugly Fly Number 2 (see Chapter 6).

You will need a guide and powerboat after landing in the lower river. There are many bears along the river.

There is no lodging on Kamishak—fly-ins only.

Nearby lodging and services include:

→ Homer Air. Air taxi from Homer, AK.

→ Rainbow King Lodge. Excellent full-service lodge with daily fly-outs; expensive.

KANEKTOK RIVER

Use a commercial airline to Dillingham or Bethel. These towns are about one hour by jet west of Anchorage. Then take a floatplane to the lake or wheelplane to the village. Not accessible by car.

This area is famous for float fishing and beautiful scenery. It offers excellent fly fishing conditions for all five species of salmon plus rainbows, char and graylings.

The water quality is excellent for sight fishing. The river drains from mountains, not glacial waters. It has a gravel bottom with many shallow braids and many fish. The number of medium-sized rainbows is very high. The native fish, char and grayling, in the upper river, are very good here. There are large sea-run char in the lower river.

The following services offer transport to Kanektok:

→ Freshwater Adventures, Inc. Air taxi.

→ Kanektok River Safaris. Unguided spike camp.

→ Kuskokwim Aviation. Air taxi.

→ Ultimate Rivers. Guided float trips.

KASILOF RIVER

The Kasilof is located on the Kenai Peninsula, with easy road access (about three hours driving) south from Anchorage.

Or you can fly into the town of Kenai and rent a car or stay at one of the nearby lodges.

The water here is opaque, because it is glacially fed. So it requires large and bright flies working near the bottom.

King salmon are very good in the early summer; silvers and dolly varden are good in the late summer and early fall. Sockeyes are plentiful, but difficult to catch.

Effective flies include the Chartreuse Everglow Fly for kings; Fuchsia Bunny Fly for sockeyes, chum and silvers; and Sam's Ugly Numbers 1 and 2 for dolly varden (see Chapter 6 on flies to take).

Lodging includes:

➠ Deep Creek Fishing Club (south of Kasilof). Full-service lodge; moderate prices.

➠ Great Alaska Fish Camp (on Kenai). Full-service lodge; offers guides on Kasilof and Kenai; moderate prices.

There are also many guiding services in Soldotna.

KENAI RIVER

One of the few large rivers easily accessible by car, this river is about three hours south of Anchorage and has outstanding scenery. The glacial, opaque water is a beautiful, aquamarine color. Two portions, the upper Kenai and lower Kenai, each have unique characteristics and quality fishing. As a result, it can be very crowded at key spots on the river and there may be parking problems and heavy traffic on the highways.

The upper river is especially scenic, with the river meandering through forested mountains. The emerald and aquama-

rine water contrasted with the green, forested mountains makes for excellent photographs on sunny days. Wonderful for drifting in a boat or raft fishing.

The upper Kenai offers excellent sockeye runs in late June and silver runs in late August through September. Excellent rainbows, arctic char and dolly varden are available here. My personal record for rainbow in Alaska was 8 pounds and 33 inches on the upper Kenai River using Sam's Ugly Fly Number 1 (see Chapter 6). There are not too many grayling in the main river. The upper river is currently closed to king salmon fishing. The unique, ice-free Kenai allows fishing in winter for char and silver salmon.

The lower Kenai has slow tidal waters and has many accessible spots on the river. An early run of king salmon comes in May and June and a second run in July and August. Silver salmon run in May, June, September and October. Sockeyes run from May through August. The Moose River flows into the lower Kenai making it a popular holding area for salmon.

In the lower Kenai, kings are sometimes unpredictable, but they can be very large. The record king was taken from the lower Kenai and weighed 97 pounds. There are sometimes fishing restrictions and no-fishing days. Ask the lodge manager or guide before your trip. Be prepared for heavy crowds during peak salmon runs, especially along wadable portions of the river that are accessible by car. Many commercial guides and float concessions can be found in this area. It may be difficult to find a guide for fly fishing during salmon season when conventional gear fishing is common, because most are using back trolling and drifting with attractor lures and conventional fishing gear.

Lodging and services include:

➟ Alaska River Company. Guides.

➟ Alaska Trout Fitters. Guides.

➟ Great Alaska Fish Camp. Excellent full-service lodge with daily guide service and optional fly-outs available; guides to upper and lower rivers. (See Appendix 4.)

➟ Kenai Lake Lodge. Rooms.

➟ R.W.'s Fishing. Guides only.

➟ Timberline Guide Service. Guides only.

KIKLUKH RIVER

This picturesque river, located east of Anchorage, can be reached by taking a commercial jet to Cordova, then a wheeled light airplane to Kiklukh. This area is not accessible by car.

This is an outstanding clear water river for catching huge silver salmon—up to 20 pounds and more. It is considered one of the best silver waters in Alaska. It is shallow, averaging 2 to 3 feet deep, which allows sight fishing from shore. No boats are allowed. Late August to September is the peak period; it tapers off in October. Be prepared for rain. Only artificial lures may be used through September 14. Also a good place for sockeye salmon from late June through early July.

Lodging is offered by the following:

➡ Alaska Gulf Coast Adventures. Camp Kiklukh is a full-service, guided tent camp; wheeled fly-outs; pickup from Cordova; low to moderate price. (See Appendix 4.)

KODIAK ISLAND RIVERS

Kodiak Island has many fishable rivers, including 20 major river systems. But for purposes of this book, a summary of selected and representative rivers is discussed. A major virtue of Kodiak is that the fishable rivers are all close to the Cook Inlet waters where halibut can be readily caught, so going for salmon in rivers and halibut in the ocean while staying at the same location is feasible.

The town of Kodiak is the hub of Kodiak Island and is located to the south of Anchorage, about one hour by air. The towns of Homer, Seldovia and Seward provide boat service to Kodiak, including transporting automobiles.

A short road system exists on Kodiak Island that provides access to local streams, but the majority of rivers are only accessible by floatplane. Overall, Kodiak Island has excellent salmon fishing, but the timing is limited to shorter periods for most salmon, compared to mainland Alaska.

In Kodiak, there are both hotels and bed and breakfasts. It is important to know that if the weather is bad in Kodiak the air taxis may be grounded, so you may not be able to get off the island. It is a good idea to have backup lodging in Kodiak arranged, or be prepared to wait in the Kodiak airport terminal. Lodging in Kodiak includes the Westmark Kodiak Hotel.

AMERICAN RIVER ON KODIAK

This river is located about 10 miles south of Kodiak and is accessible by car. You can rent a car at Kodiak or drive from Anchorage and use a ferry boat to go to Kodiak Island. This is a very good area to find silver salmon and chum salmon in late summer.

The following lodging is available:

➥ Several inns and B&Bs in Kodiak. Drive to American River.

➥ Kalsin Inn Ranch. Full-service lodge; guides.

➠ Alaska State Parks. Camping.

AYAKULIK RIVER ON KODIAK

Located about 85 miles southwest of Kodiak, this river offers excellent king salmon fishing in early June. Also, there is good sockeye salmon fishing in late June and July, silver salmon in September, and dollies from June through August. You can access this area by floatplane from Kodiak.

The following lodging and services are available:

➠ Kodiak National Wildlife Refuge (in Kodiak). Cabins.

➠ Kodiak Adventures and Ayakulik Camp. Guide service.

➠ Uyak Air. Air taxi.

➠ Sea Hawk Air. Air taxi.

BUSKIN RIVER ON KODIAK

This river is one of the few accessible by car from Kodiak. It is very good for catching sockeye salmon from late June to mid-July. The silver salmon run is good during the second half of September, and chums and dollies are also available. There is no king salmon fishing allowed. The sight fishing is good here.

You can find lodging and other services at the following:

➠ Buskin River Inn. Lodging and guide service.

➠ Alaska State Park. Campgrounds.

DOG SALMON RIVER ON KODIAK

Located about 80 miles southwest of Kodiak, this river is accessed by floatplane from Kodiak. There is excellent chum salmon fishing in mid-summer and good silver salmon fishing in late summer. Fishing for king salmon is not allowed. This land is private land and requires a use permit through Koniag Inc.

The following lodging and services are available:

→ Kodiak National Wildlife Refuge. Cabins.

→ Sea Hawk Air. Air taxi.

→ Uyak Air Service. Air taxi.

KARLUK RIVER ON KODIAK

The Karluk River is located about 75 miles southwest of Kodiak and is accessed by floatplane or raft. This river is famous for its excellent king salmon fishing in late June and early July. Also, sockeye salmon are available in late June and late July, and silver salmon in late September. There are dollies from May through November.

The following lodging and services are available:

→ Karluk Lodge. Full-service lodge.

→ Kodiak National Wildlife Refuge. Cabins.

→ Sea Hawk Air. Air taxi.

→ Uyak Air. Air taxi.

PASAGSHAK RIVER ON KODIAK

This river, accessible by car, is known for very good silver salmon fishing. It is located 25 miles south of Kodiak. The river is clear and easy to fish. Large silvers up to 20 pounds run in September. Sockeyes run from late June through early July and dollies in May and July through October. King fishing is prohibited.

The following lodging is available:
- → Alaska State Park. Campground.
- → Kalsin Inn Ranch. Lodging and guiding.
- → Kodiak. Inns and B&B's.

SALTERY RIVER ON KODIAK

This river is known for its silver salmon in late September. Sockeyes are available in early July and dollies in May and July through October. It has clear water, is easily fishable, but the road to the river requires a four-wheel drive vehicle.

The following lodging is available:
- → Kodiak. Inns and B&Bs.
- → Saltery Lake Lodge. Full-service lodging.

UGANIK RIVER ON KODIAK

Located in the northwest section of Kodiak Island, access to this river is by floatplane from Kodiak. It offers outstanding silver salmon fishing from late August through early September. Other species available include sockeye (late June through early July), chum, pink salmon and char.

Lodging and services in the area include:
Kodiak National Wildlife Refuge. Cabins.

Wilderness Air. Air taxi.

KVICHAK RIVER

The Kvichak is a major river in the southwest region of Alaska. It flows out of Iliamna Lake to Bristol Bay, about 30 miles north of King Salmon commercial airport. Transportation to Kvichak is by floatplane. There is no auto access.

This is a big river that requires a boat to get to fishing waters. Fish in tributaries flowing into Kvichak. Fly fishing is difficult, but can be done at lake outlets. On the main river, most people use conventional gear with spoons and plugs. This river is excellent for catching rainbows in early summer and late fall, though the weather can be a problem in the fall; other fish include char, grayling, chum, and sockeye and silver salmon.

Lodging and services include:

➡ Alaska Rainbow Lodge. Full-service lodge; guides; daily fly-outs; expensive.

➡ No See Um Lodge. Full-service lodge; daily fly-outs; expensive.

➡ Ole Creek Lodge. Full-service lodge; guides; moderate.

MORAINE CREEK

Located in Katmai National Preserve with access by local air taxi. Get here by flying from Anchorage to Iliamna or King Salmon and take advantage of outstanding fall rainbow trout fishing.

The water is clear, making this creek popular for sight fishing for rainbows. Early summer and late summer to fall are best—big rainbows emerge out of lakes to seek salmon eggs and flesh. Also popular for char and grayling fishing.

The following lodging and services are available:

➡ Angler's Alibi Tent Camp. Full-service camp with fly-out options; low to moderately priced.

➡ Katmailand, Inc. Cabins and lodge; guides.

⟶ No See Um Lodge. Full-service luxury lodge; fly-out services; expensive.

NAKNEK RIVER

This river is located in the southwest and access is into the town of King Salmon, about a one-hour jet flight southwest from Anchorage. It has excellent salmon and trout fishing. Stay in King Salmon and take daily guided boat trips.

This clear-water river flows from Naknek Lake in Katmai National Park, through King Salmon, then drains into Bristol Bay about 30 miles west of Naknet Lake.

It offers excellent salmon and trout fishing; big rainbows and large char are available in spring and fall through October. It has very good king salmon in early summer and silver salmon in late summer.

For flies, I recommend Black Woolly Buggers, Sam's Ugly Numbers 1 and 2 and Olive Woolhead Sculpins for rainbows; Sockeye Orange Fly, Chartreuse Everglow Fly and Fuchsia Bunny Fly for salmon (see Chapter 6 for flies to take).

The following lodging and services are available:

⟶ King Ko Inn. Full-service inn with restaurant on premises; guiding available; low prices.

⟶ Mark Emery Guiding Services

⟶ Morrison Guide Services

⟶ No See Um Lodge. Full-service luxury lodge; guides; daily fly-outs; expensive.

⟶ Ponderosa Inn. B&B with all meals available; inexpensive.

→ Quinnat Landing Hotel. Full-service hotel; guiding available, including optional trips to Katmai National Park; moderately priced.

NEWHALEN RIVER

There are tremendous runs of sockeye and rainbow on the Newhalen. It flows into Lake Iliamna on the north side, just adjacent to Iliamna commercial airport, about one hour from Anchorage by turboprop aircraft. It is partially road accessible from the town of Iliamna, which you must fly into. Use local lodging and guide service.

The water of this river is almost clear blue. It is excellent for fly fishing rainbows in September and October and char and grayling. There are huge runs of sockeyes in early to mid-July just below the falls. Also, many chum, king, pink and silver salmon inhabit these waters.

The following lodging is available:

→ Rainbow King Lodge. Full-service guided lodge with daily fly-outs to privately leased space below falls.

NUSHAGAK RIVER

Flows into Nushagak Bay and central Bristol Bay, about 300 miles southwest of Anchorage. There are no roads to this river. Fly to Dillingham and stay in a lodge or bed and breakfast in town. Use a guide to visit the numerous native villages along the river. Floatplanes are available from Dillingham or Iliamna to various spots along the river.

Clear water and many gravel bars make fly fishing easy on the Nushagak. All five species of salmon, rainbows, char and grayling are available. Silvers, rainbows, grayling and char are upriver in late summer and fall.

The lower Nushagak is an excellent spot for kings from third week in June to mid-July. Portage Creek is especially popular; visitors must fly in and set up tents. With a good guide, you can average between three to ten kings per day.

The following lodging and services are available:

➡ Freshwater Adventures Inc. Air taxi.

➡ Ultimate Rivers. Spike camp fishing.

➡ Western Alaska Sportfishing. Serves the upper river.

RUSSIAN RIVER

The Russian River is located on the Kenai Peninsula, about two and one-half hours drive south of Anchorage. The drive is very scenic, but the area can be very crowded during mid-summer months.

The water is clear, compared to the turquoise of the Kenai River. There is no road access above the outlet at Kenai. Hiking trails line the river and many animals, including bears and moose can be seen (see Chapter 15 on bears).

A famous location is at the confluence of the Russian with the Kenai. It has easy road access, which results in a large number of elbow-to-elbow fisherpeople, referred to as the "combat zone" during salmon runs. But fishing is very effective because of easy wading and a large concentration of salmon.

Sockeye fishing is very good in mid-summer, silver fishing is good in late summer, and rainbow and dolly fishing is good in summer and fall.

Effective flies for this river include Sockeye Orange, Fuchsia Bunny Fly for salmon and Black Woolly Bugger, Olive Woolhead Sculpin and Sam's Ugly Numbers 1 and 2. See Chapter 6 on flies to take.

The following lodging and services are available:

➥ Chugach National Forest. Cabins.

➥ Great Alaska Fish Camp. Excellent full-service lodge; daily guide service; optional fly-outs.

➥ Kenai Lake Lodge. Cabins.

SHIP CREEK

Ship Creek is near downtown Anchorage and is within walking distance from downtown hotels. By car, go to 1st Avenue and Loop Road. This area is very crowded during salmon season because of its close proximity to the city. It is a nice diversion for those with a few hours to spare in the city. Salmon can be seen just below the dam, which is a no-fishing zone. Fishing is allowed below the Department of Fish and Game marker wire.

Both sides of the water are accessible by road. Kings are available until the river is closed; contact the local Department of Fish and Game at (907) 267-2218 for the latest rules.

The water is generally clear except during heavy rains. Silver salmon run in late summer through October. There are some pinks here in even years, and chums and char.

The following lodging is available in Anchorage:

→ Captain Cook Hotel, Hilton Hotel, Sheraton Hotel. Expensive.

→ Comfort Inn. Moderate.

→ Westmark Hotel. Moderate.

→ Other Motels and Bed and Breakfast Lodging. Low to moderate prices.

SITUK RIVER

Located near Yakutat, this river is about one hour by jet southeast from Anchorage. You can drive from Yakutat or take a floatplane five miles to the east.

This clear-water river is world famous for steelhead trout in late fall and early winter. It is also very good for sockeye salmon in early summer, king salmon in mid-summer and silver salmon in late summer. Large rainbow trout arrive in late summer and fall. Check with local lodges or guides for the best times to visit.

The following lodging and services are available:

→ Blue Heron Inn. Lodging and guide service.

→ Glacier Bear Lodge. Full-service lodge and guide service.

→ Yakutat Bay and River Charters. Guiding.

→ Yakutat Ranger District. Cabin rentals.

TALACHULITNA RIVER

Located north of Anchorage, the Talachlitna is reached by floatplane or wheelplane. It is not accessible by car. The air taxi takes 30 minutes from Merrill Field, near downtown Anchorage. This river combines fast, rough water with smooth, wadable water.

Clear water makes this river ideal for fly fishing and the surrounding forests and gorges offer a beautiful setting. It is an excellent river for floating. The upper river is slow and shallow, but there are areas of rapids and canyons along the way. Requires experienced boaters.

This river has strong runs of king and silver salmon and rainbows, although they are somewhat medium-sized compared to the large rainbows found in other rivers around Iliamna Lake. Catch and release rainbows. The upper river is good for catching grayling.

Lodging and transportation in this area include:

→ Ketchum Air Service. Air taxi.

→ Regal Air. Air taxi.

→ Rust's Flying Service. Air taxi.

→ Talaview Resorts. Full-service lodge; guides; low-to-moderate prices (see Appendix 4 for specific recommendations).

TALARIK CREEK

Talarik Creek flows into Iliamna Lake 25 miles west of the town of Iliamna. There is commercial airplane service available from Anchorage to Iliamna.

The lower Tularik Creek is world famous for rainbow that

come up from Iliamna Lake to feed on salmon eggs and flesh during spawning season. Sockeye salmon are abundant during early summer and late summer to early fall.

To catch rainbow trout, use Black Woolly Bugger, Olive Woolhead Sculpin and Sam's Ugly Numbers 1 and 2 (see Chapter 6 on flies to take).

The following lodging and services are available:

➡ Iliamna Airport Hotel. Guide service.

➡ Iliamna Air Taxi. Air taxi.

➡ Rainbow King Lodge. Luxury full-service lodge in Iliamna; guides; daily floatplane service; expensive.

TOGIAK RIVER

Located on western Bristol Bay, the Togiak is about one hour by jet from Anchorage to Dillingham, then by floatplane to Togiak river. There is no road access. It is an easy float trip by raft to the lower river, then return on the floatplane.

This river is scenic, with clear water and excellent king, silver and char fishing. Kings enter around June 10 and peak the first week in July. Chum and pinks are good in July; silvers are outstanding in August. Fly fishing is difficult; most people use conventional spinning and casting gear.

The following services are available:

➡ Freshwater Adventures, Inc. Air taxi.

➡ Ultimate Rivers. Guide service.

UPPER SUSITNA AND TALKEETNA RIVERS

These rivers are accessible by car from Parks Highway; or take a boat from the town of Talkeetna, about three hours north of Anchorage. This is a big river with no sight fishing except in upriver tributaries. Deshka and Alexander Creek are accessible by riverboat services along Parks Highway.

This river was created from glacier runoff. It is generally opaque, but feeder tributaries may run clear, allowing for sight fishing. The river is fast, so the desirable tributaries are accessed by powerful jetboats.

Fish for rainbows, dolly varden, char, sockeyes, pinks, chum and silvers. Kings and silvers can be very good here, especially early in the season. Portage Creek and Whiskers Creek offer very good king, silver and grayling fishing.

The following inexpensive lodging and services are available in Talkeetna:

➟ Mahay's Riverboat Service. Guiding.

➟ River Beauty B&B. Lodging.

➟ Talkeetna Motel. Rooms, restaurant and lounge.

➟ Talkeetna Riverboat Service. Guiding.

➟ Three Rivers Accommodations. Cabins.

Chapter

6

TEN FLIES TO TAKE

In the previous chapters, we discussed how to select your desired species, rivers, and lodging and camps. In this chapter you will decide which flies to take by:

⬥ Identifying the most effective flies for catching your desired species (see Appendix 1).

⬥ Narrowing your list of flies down to 10 or fewer.

For my earliest fly fishing trips to Alaska, I spent a lot of money buying flies of many types and sizes. Then I learned how to tie flies, which helped me save money.

But I ended up overusing this new cost-saving skill. I made so many flies, enough to cover all contingencies per the recommended fly lists from various lodges, that I didn't save any money. And I wound up with too many unused flies— about 90 percent of the flies I tied for a trip were never used.

After years of this experience, I now know that most fish in Alaska, and elsewhere in the world, are somewhat predictable at any given time and location. I now find that the most cost-effective approach to deciding on flies to take is as follows:

1. If you are going to a river with no lodge or guide, use the list of flies for your target species given in Appendix 1.

2. If an experienced guide or escort is not available, contact one of the fly shops in Anchorage by letter, fax or phone and ask them to comment on and prioritize your fly list for a specific river and for the time of year that you are going. Preferably 10 or fewer of the most effective flies should be taken.

3. If you are going to a lodge or plan to be guided, call the lodge or guide about 30 days before the trip. Ask for an update on the flies that are most likely to work, and for size, color and other specifications. They should be able to narrow down the five most effective flies and the best hook sizes for each.

4. If you are interested in catching a large variety of species, ask about the top 10 flies for the trip.

When I go to Alaska, my objective is to catch the maximum number of different species in a limited time. So I prepare the following 10 flies to meet my objective. This set of flies is generally useful during the peak of the summer season, which is mid-July for most species of salmon and native fish in all rivers of southcentral and southwest Alaska.

Again, I recommend contacting the lodge, camp manager or guide shortly before the trip to confirm the best type of flies for the scheduled arrival time. They may try to sell you their custom-designed fly, but keep insisting on their opinion of the list you prepared.

BLACK WOOLLY BUGGER

(Options for Flash Tail, Pearl Body or Chartreuse Body)

For king salmon, chum salmon, silver salmon, pink salmon, rainbow trout, arctic char, dolly varden and arctic grayling.

Start the thread, leaving head space behind eye. Wrap

Hook:	TMC 300, sizes 2 to 10
Weight:	0.030-inch lead
Thread:	Black 6/0
Tail:	Black marabou
Body:	Large black chenille
Hackle:	Black saddle
Options:	Crystal flash added to tail
	Black pearl chenille on body
	Chartreuse chenille on body
	Bead eyes

thread along shank to bend. Tie in marabou tail, about length of shank. Wrap marabou along shank, leave head space behind eye, tie in. Trim excess. Wrap thread back to bend. Tie in hackle tip. Tie in chenille. Wrap chenille around shank toward eye, leaving head space. Palmer the hackle forward, laying in between chenille turns. Tie off hackle stem at front of chenille. Form head with thread and whip finish. Option: replace head with bead eyes tied in using figure eights.

CHARTREUSE EVERGLOW

For king salmon, chum salmon, pink salmon and silver salmon.

After applying lead to shank, cover shank with yarn to build diameter to match diameter of Everglow Tubing. Tie at back at bend of hook, leaving straggling Everglow fibers to create a tail. Tie off. Reattach thread behind eye. Tie front part of tubing, leaving room behind eye for wing. Tie bucktail underwing then Everglow overwing with wing length just beyond bend of

Hook:	Mustad No. 3407 or equivalent salt water fly hook, sizes 3/0 to 2
Weight:	0.035-inch lead
Thread:	Chartreuse 3/0
Body:	Yarn to cover lead and build body, then cover with Chartreuse Everglow Tubing (Cascade Fly Supply, Oregon), or contact author
Hackle:	Chartreuse saddle
Underwing:	Chartreuse bucktail
Overwing:	Chartreuse Everglow wing material

hook and matching the length of tail. Attach saddle hackle and make three wraps. Cover head with thread and whip finish.

CREAM ELK HAIR CADDIS

For arctic grayling, rainbow trout, arctic char and dolly varden.

Hook:	TMC 100 or equivalent standard dry fly hook, sizes 8 to 12
Thread:	Light Tan 3/0
Rib:	Fine gold wire
Body:	Hare's mask dubbing
Hackle:	Brown
Wing:	Bleached elk hair (cream shade if possible)

   Start thread at the shank about one eye diameter away
from the eye. Tie in gold wire. Lift wire from shank, take
thread down to bend. Secure thread. Dub the shank up to
thread starting point behind eye. Tie in hackle about two eye
diameters behind eye. Trim stem. Spiral (palmer) the hackle
to bend, using about seven turns. Grasp wire and make one
tight turn over hackle tip. Add three more turns of wire over
the tip and spiral the wire up through hackle, working to eye.
Secure wire with thread. Trim wire and hackle ends. Comb
elk hair and stack to even ends. Hold against shank with tips
slightly beyond length of hook. Holding hair over shank, trim
end of hair just in front of eye. Move hair bunch slightly back
so blunt end is just behind eye. Tie in hair end and whip finish. Trim elk hair.

FUCHSIA BUNNY (AKA CERISE BUNNY)

For chum salmon, king salmon, pink salmon and silver salmon.

Add lead to shank from bend to two eye-widths behind eye. Secure lead, leaving thread at bend. Tie in one rabbit strip,

Hook:	Mustad 9672 or equivalent 3X long streamer hook, size 2
Weight:	0.035-inch lead
Thread:	Fuchsia or Black 3/0
Tail and Body:	Fuchsia rabbit fur cut into 3/16-inch strips

leaving tail length equal to shank length. Take thread forward. Wrap remaining rabbit strip in tight spirals around shank (rotating vise makes this simpler), taking care to not pinch hairs while rotating. To create head, bunch the spirals tighter. Tie off, whip finish.

GOLD RIBBED HARE'S EAR NYMPH

For arctic grayling, rainbow trout, arctic char and dolly varden.

Wrap thread, starting behind eye, leaving some head space. Wrap thread to bend. Tie in guard hair tail. Tie gold ribbing wire, leave loose. Add weight to shank. Dub a cigar-shaped abdomen, about two-thirds the length of shank. Wind gold wire around abdomen up to end of abdomen and tie in. Tie in turkey quill wingcase in front of abdomen, leave loose. Dub in thorax. Pull wingcase over the thorax and tie down, trim. Form head

Hook:	TMC 3769 or equivalent heavy wire hook, sizes 8 to 12
Weight:	0.015-inch thick
Thread:	Black, 6/0
Tail:	Guard hairs from hare's mask
Ribbing:	Oval Gold Tinsel, small or fine
Abdomen:	Hare's mask dubbing
Thorax:	Hare's mask dubbing
Wing Case:	Brown mottled turkey quill

with thread, whip finish. Pluck out some dubbing on underside to give it a "buggy" look.

OLIVE WOOLHEAD SCULPIN

For rainbow trout, arctic char, dolly varden and arctic grayling.

Hook:	Mustad 9672 or equivalent 3X streamer hook, sizes 2 to 6
Weight:	0.030-inch lead
Thread:	Black 6/0
Tail:	Olive rabbit strip, 3/16-inch wide
Ribbing:	15-pound monofilament
Body:	Black or olive chenille, large
Fins:	Grouse body feathers
Wing:	Rabbit strip, 3/16-inch wide
Head:	Olive wool

Wrap lead around shank, rear two-thirds. Tie down lead at both ends. Tie in rabbit strip tail with tail length equal to length of shank. Do not cut rabbit strip, to be used for body later. First tie in the ribbing line; monofilament. Tie in chenille. Take thread forward to head. Cover lead portion with chenille, leaving large space for wool head. Hold rabbit strip on top of shank and work in monofilament line through the hair fibers, securing the strip to shank. Tie in both rabbit strip and chenille and trim. Tie in grouse body feather, one each on a side, so they point straight out from shank. Add small amounts of wool to head area of shank, similar to adding spun deer hair for Muddler heads. Whip finish. Clip head shape, apply thin cement to top of head.

PARACHUTE ADAMS

For rainbow trout, arctic char, dolly varden and arctic grayling.

Wrap front half of shank and tie in wing. Wing should be three-quarters of shank length. Tie in hackles, leaving short section of bare stem from tie-down point to start of barbs. Wind back to end of shank and tie in tail. Dub onto thread. Wind dubbing body to point behind the wing. Create post of parachute wing by wrapping thread around base. Wind hackles, concave

Hook:	**Mustad 94840 or similar, sizes 10 to 18**
Thread:	**Black 6/0**
Wing:	**White calf tail (about 15 strands, varying with size of hook)**
Body:	**Muskrat dubbing**
Hackle:	**One brown and one grizzly dry fly**
Tail:	**Brown and grizzly hackle fibers mixed (about 10 strands, varying with size of hook)**

side down, horizontally around base of wing. Make three turns for each hackle. Dub underneath and in front of wing and wrap head. Whip finish.

SAM'S UGLY NO. 1
(Simulated Salmon Egg Cluster)

For rainbow trout, arctic char, dolly varden and arctic grayling.

Using the monofilament leader, tie a "Snell" knot on the shank of the hook (actually, any strong knot on the shank will do, but the Snell is the strongest). Create a loop by creating slack in the leader that goes from the knot through the eye of the hook. Into this loop insert the various cut yarn colors that may be appealing to the trout. Pull down on the line to lock in the yarn. Yarn can be replaced in the field by simply feeding the tippet into the eye and opening the loop. Alternate colored

Hook:	Mustad 92553, sizes 1/0 to 6
Tippet:	15-pound monofilament leader
Wing:	Simulated egg sack using one-inch long multi-colored Glo-Bug yarn (baseline fly has White, Apricot Supreme and Flame, but alternate colors can be tried)

yarns can be quickly inserted.

Yarn can be obtained at most fly supply stores, but the author's preferred yarn is made by the Bug Shop, 20922 Dodson Lane, Anderson, CA 96007. Use with a sinker or a sink tip line to get the fly to the bottom of the river. This simulates a salmon egg cluster that is drifting downstream from the spawning redd.

An optional design is to tie in yarn like normal Glo-Bug, but this becomes a permanent fly and the yarn is not replaceable in the field.

SAM'S UGLY No. 2
(Champagne Glo-Bug)

For rainbow trout, arctic char, dolly varden and arctic grayling.

Cut three pieces of Glo-Bug yarn, about one inch long. Attach thread to center of shank. Place cut yarn on top of shank. Wrap thread around yarn in middle, wrapping four to six times, holding yarn in position on top. Pull yarn back from eye, wrap thread directly in front of yarn about eight times, whip finish. Hold yarn vertically, pulling hard up from hook. Cut yarn all at once

Hook:	Mustad 9174 or equivalent 3X short, 1X strong, sizes 6 to 8
Thread:	Kevlar or Flymaster Plus or similar very strong
Body:	Glo-Bug yarn, Champagne Pink

in a slight arc, leaving about 1/4-inch length of yarn on hook. Fluff yarn around, making a ball. (Note that size of simulated egg determines how much to cut on yarn.)

SOCKEYE ORANGE

For sockeye salmon.

Tie thread at bend, tie tinsel, take thread forward to head. Wrap tinsel over shank forward to head. Attach hackle with

Hook:	TMC 7989 or equivalent salmon wet fly, sizes 6 to 8
Thread:	Black, 6/0
Body:	Flat silver tinsel
Hackle:	Orange saddle
Wing:	Black squirrel tail

three turns. Tie off. Attach wing, create head with thread, whip finish.

Additional flies can be considered and made. Check with your destination guide. See Appendix 2 for a wider selection of flies and see Appendix 6 for specific patterns and materials for other flies.

Chapter

7

THE MONEY SAVING STAGE:
AFFORDABILITY

So far you have developed a plan that includes your objective fish, waters, time of year, lodging or camping and necessary equipment. Now we will focus on ways you can cut costs further.

WHAT IS AFFORDABILITY?

The late Sam Winston of the successful tire business wanted to be first at the remote, unfished waters of the world, whether they were in Argentina, Eastern Russia or elsewhere. The threshold of affordability was high for Sam—the finest luxury lodges in premier locations worldwide at the best time of year were affordable.

In contrast to Sam Winston, there are fly fishers who go to Alaska several times each summer, stay with friends, borrow equipment and bring supplies from home to save money. To them, affordability means the lowest possible cost to get to fish.

Another fellow goes to Argentina several times each season, almost monthly. He has dedicated what remains of his life to this pursuit, budgeting as needed to meet his goal. For him to afford this way of life, everything else must take lower priority.

I saw a fisherman at a telephone in Anchorage airport, calling as many lodges as possible at the last minute, seeking the best price for unsold spaces at fishing locations. He risked not being able to find a discounted space, but accepted that risk knowing the chance of finding a bargain was worth the savings. Affordability means taking a gamble with the hope of finding a major cost reduction.

All of these people have been able to travel to faraway places for fly fishing because they made up their minds that this objective was a priority in their life. Affordability was a challenging problem to be solved in pursuit of a more important goal. Cost was not a limitation, but a variable to be adjusted.

The most expensive arrangements are full-service lodges with first-class accommodations. At the time of this writing, high-end facilities having dedicated fly-out aircraft or helicopters to service customers could cost up to $1000 per day, or $7000 per week.

But some lodges offer close to the same excellent quality and personal service for up to 40 percent less. They are able to operate more economically because they have more customers and larger aircraft that carry more people at the same time.

LOW COST OPTIONS:

Special Discounts

Some lodges will drop their prices in the spring to fill unusual vacancy situations. Prices drop as much as 25 to 50 percent below advertised list prices. Stay in touch with agents or specialists who maintain contact with these sources. Because there are over 250 lodges and guides in the premium Bristol Bay region, it would be difficult and expensive to do this on your own.

Group Discounts

Traveling as part of a group is an effective way to save money. If you can organize a group, the larger the better, you can save significantly on air travel and ground facilities. This package planning must be done early in the year to assure obtaining a facility that can handle a large group.

Partial Week Stays

Another way to cut the cost of lodging is to find a partial week arrangement. Staying three full days and two nights (early morning arrival and late evening departure) can qualify you for lower rates than you would receive if staying for a full week. (See Appendix 3 for lodges offering partial week stays.)

Unexpected Vacancies

Sometimes lodges have unexpected vacancies

created by people who stay for only a few days out of their reserved week. If you are flexible, let the lodge manager select those days for you and make an offer to occupy at a special rate.

Remember that most lodges try to stay filled to full capacity and keep their staffs busy serving clients. That is the best way for them to cover their high, fixed operating costs.

EVEN LOWER COST OPTIONS:

Group Float Trips

Sharing expenses by teaming for an unguided, tent camping trip using floats or rafts can be very inexpensive. Someone in the group needs to be skilled in managing floats and camp setups. If you don't know the difference between Class I and V rivers, are not experienced in wilderness camping, or are not physically fit for the extreme rigors of the Alaskan environment, do not attempt an unguided float trip.

Forest Service Cabins

Staying at forest service cabins and bringing your own supplies can also be inexpensive. You must access many of these remote cabins by float plane. (For references, see Appendices 2 and 3.)

DO-IT-YOURSELF (ALMOST FREE)

Fishing near Anchorage or along the Alaskan road system without using guides can be very low cost. (See Appendix 4 for details.)

HOW TO SAVE MONEY ON TRAVEL

For many people, the major cost for a trip to Alaska is getting to their destination lodge, camp or river. The next step in refining your plan is learning how to get there while saving money. Getting to the preferred rivers in Alaska from the lower 48 states or other countries takes several airplanes. The key to reducing air travel costs is to seek information about alternative airfares.

The following examples show fares based on actual quoted prices by airlines and travel agencies in the early summer of 1996. These are shown for illustrative purposes only and may not be in effect at the time you seek to book flights.

STANDARD LIST PRICE AIRFARE

All airlines have listed prices for standard, refundable, changeable ticketing at any time of the week. These are best for business travelers who have no choice but to make last minute flight preparations and may have to change flights before or during the trip.

From the Los Angeles area, a quoted list price for an unrestricted, roundtrip to Anchorage, Alaska is $834.

PLAN AHEAD DISCOUNTED AIRFARES

If you can arrange to travel on certain days and purchase tickets in advance, the prices can drop significantly. For example, traveling on Tuesday, Wednesday and Saturday is cheaper than traveling on the peak demand days of Monday, Friday and Sunday. Several airlines quoted a fare of $438 roundtrip to Anchorage for these non-peak days.

With travel further restricted to late Friday and all day

Saturday, and the ticket purchased at least 21 days in advance, one quoted roundtrip price was only $299.

OTHER DISCOUNTED AIRFARES

A fact in the travel business that is not well known by the traveling public is that airfares are negotiable with the airlines. The airlines will drop prices even below published discount fares if a group (15 or more, for example) requests a quote from the carrier. These are non-changeable, non-refundable restricted air tickets. A more sizable group will result in further reductions.

Sometimes there are hidden fares that are not readily displayed on travel agency computers. These require further research and effort by travel agents to find the best fares for certain city combinations. The reason for these fares is that cities on the way to Anchorage may have slack periods and offer promotional fares to induce travelers to pass through them.

The bottom line is that the greatest savings are obtained by agents who will work for you and look for the maximum savings. And the use of quantity discounts with group travel helps significantly.

ASK LODGE OR PACKAGE PROMOTER

On occasion, the lodge manager or float trip concession owner arranges a package with a travel agent in Alaska for special airfare discounts. When requesting a single airfare within Alaska, it is difficult to get significant discounts. But when a package arrangement is made between the lodge owner and a travel agency in Anchorage, a substantial discount from the lowest posted airfare is possible. It never hurts to ask and you just might be rewarded.

FREQUENT FLIER MILEAGE— NO COST, BUT CAUTION!

Using frequent flier mileage to cover air transportation to Alaska is the least expensive way to get there. However, some warnings on using the frequent flier system to Alaska are worth mentioning.

It takes a significant number of credits to get to Anchorage, even in coach class. If you have other international destinations you are considering visiting, such as Argentina or New Zealand, you might save your frequent flier miles for these destinations, as they rarely offer significantly discounted airfares. Compare the cost for discounted fares to Anchorage versus discounted fares internationally. It may be an advantage to pay for discounted Alaskan air transportation and save the points for other world destinations where such discounts are not available.

Here is another important consideration. There are many people who want to use their frequent flier miles for Alaska. The airlines know it and sharply restrict the number of seats on airplanes during the peak summer season. One would think that by reserving a month or two before the trip, such seats would be available. But many people with frequent flier points have the same idea, so they call and reserve early. I usually call up to a year ahead.

The airlines' computers are programmed to not allow reservations before a set period prior to the flight, typically 330 days before the departure day. So, stay in touch with the airline to find out the earliest exact date and time the computers will allow you to make reservations. Calling the airline at midnight in the time zone where the airline's computers are located and after the computers are reset to allow new reservations will place you earlier in the queue.

LOCAL AIRLINES FROM ANCHORAGE TO THE RIVERS

On arriving in Anchorage, you may need to transfer to a local regional airline to get to your destination lodge or the town closest to the lodge or river you are visiting. At this time, regional carriers include ERA, Alaska and Pen Air. They use either small commercial jets or twin engine turboprop aircraft.

Almost every year, travel agencies specializing in Alaska maintain annual contracts with long-distance and regional airlines to obtain discounted prices. Contact these agencies to obtain discounted contract rates. (See Appendix 3 for information on regional transportation.)

AIR TAXIS OR SHUTTLES

Most rivers and lodges require the use of air taxis or local shuttles, which are frequently one or two engine light planes or float planes. For rivers near Anchorage, these float planes are based at Lake Hood, immediately adjacent to Anchorage International Airport. Wheeled planes are based at Merrill Field, just east of downtown Anchorage, about 25 minutes taxi ride from the International Airport.

Have the lodge make reservations for you for these flights. They can be included in the price of the destination lodge service. Also, the price may be negotiated by the lodge owner if the air service is providing a high volume of business.

CAR RENTALS

There are several car rental agencies with desks at Anchorage International Airport. My advice is to reserve your car as far ahead of time as allowed, at least six months or more. I try for about 10 months and reconfirm periodically as the date of the trip comes closer. Rates are not guaranteed until about 60 days before the trip, but reservations are allowed earlier. Shopping around for the lowest car rental rates will pay off.

For large groups, there are vans available. For off-road traveling, four-wheel drive autos are available. Some agencies charge a high surcharge for cleaning extremely soiled or muddied vehicles. To avoid these charges, use the self-cleaning car washes in Anchorage if needed.

If you wish to use frequent mileage certificates for renting a car, be certain to read the fine print concerning the days of the week the certificates can be used. Some car rental agencies will not accept the certificates for the entire rental period if allowable and unallowable days are being overlapped.

Chapter

9

HOW TO SAVE MONEY ON LODGING

Many first timers to Alaska do not get more than a short driving distance away from Anchorage. When they do get away, it is mainly for sightseeing. If local fishing and sightseeing are your objective, being based in Anchorage is fine.

There are many excellent hotels, inns, motels and other lodging throughout the city. The cost of staying in Anchorage tends to be high during the busy summer season. Daily fly-out services by air taxi are available from Lake Hood Airport, just adjacent to Anchorage International Airport. (For lodging in Anchorage, see Appendix 5 or contact the state tourism office.)

But for a serious fly fishing expedition, the best opportunities lie outside of Anchorage by at least several hours of driving or flying time. When you get away from the city, however, the choices in lodging decrease.

The following pages give categories of lodging and approximate price ranges. At the time of this writing, the summer of 1996, the prices are roughly as follows (all prices are per week and are in U.S. dollars; all food, lodging and guiding are included unless otherwise indicated; airfare to Alaska is additional):

Extremely Expensive	$6000 and above
Very Expensive	$5000–6000
Expensive	$4000–5000
Moderate	$2500–4000
Low	$1500–2500
Very Low	Under $1500

FULL-SERVICE LODGES

Full Fly-Out Lodges—Very Expensive to Extremely Expensive. These lodges are the top-of-the-line. A dedicated aircraft is assigned to each fishing party, with a maximum of three or four people to a pilot or guide. These lodges are frequently located near waters that allow convenient fishing in the event the aircraft is grounded because of bad weather; the waters are controlled by licenses from property owners, so access to them is limited. Also, the use of dedicated aircraft assures fishing in distant waters in the event the desired fish do not come close to the lodge. A lodge in this category normally offers comfortable rooms with private facilities, a large relaxing lounge, and outstanding food and service. Alcoholic beverages may be included if legal. Some locales do not allow liquor to be sold or served, but do allow you to bring your own.

Partial Fly-Out Lodges—Expensive. These cabins or lodges also have comfortable and convenient quarters, and high-quality service and meals similar to those served at the full fly-out lodges. However, aircraft are usually limited to a few days per

week or are chartered and added to the weekly cost as an option.

No Fly-Out Lodges—Moderate to Expensive. Similar to the full fly-out type of lodge, except this type of lodge is located on fishing waters, so no aircraft is necessary. Travel is restricted to local waters within a reasonable distance by boat or on foot. The location of the lodge is critical here because the choices for different fishing waters are limited. It helps to choose one of these lodges that has access to roads, in case you should wish to reach alternate rivers.

FULL-SERVICE TENT CAMPS

Full Fly-Out Camps—Expensive. These camps are similar to full fly-out lodges, but use large tents that comfortably hold two or three people per tent. There are effective heaters and some furniture within each tent. Common facilities could include a lounge and dining area. Bathing and restroom facilities are shared. Otherwise, the quality of meals and services is similar to the full fly-out lodges. Be sure, though, that you select a camp that allows good fishing nearby, just in case you cannot fly because of foul weather.

Partial Fly-Out Camps—Moderate. These camps are always located on waters that allow good fishing without the need for aircraft, but the float planes provide the option on some days for you to catch fish species not available at the base camp. Usually limited in the number of guests, possibly under 10, which allows for more personal service from the staff.

No Fly-Out Camps—Low to Moderate. These camps are similar to partial fly-out camps, but guests are restricted to local waters. Selecting the right camp and time to go is the key to a satisfying visit. Try for the camp that offers the specie you are interested in and find out the best time to go for that specie. Consider trying to negotiate a partial refund or revisit option in case the expected fish species do not arrive at the time scheduled.

FLOAT TRIPS

Guided—Low. These trips require camping at all times during the float. Guests are usually flown in by float plane with one guide and one float per group of two or three guests, and are picked up downstream, five or six days later. Guests are normally required to help operate the camp, but the primary tasks of seting up, tearing down and preparing meals are conducted by the staff. These trips are usually restricted to floatable waters that are readily fishable, somewhat limiting access to downriver tidal waters containing fresh out-of-the-sea salmon. The drawbacks to this type of trip include limited access for emergency medical assistance, sometimes special procedures are required to protect against insects, and severe wind and rain can make operations difficult.

Non-Guided Float Trips—Very Low. This type of trip requires a high degree of navigating, outdoor living, emergency, and organizing skills. It also requires that you plan the logistics of the trip and reserve equipment and transportation very early. You must coordinate with food and hardware suppliers in Anchorage or your base city, and coordinate with the air transport provider for landing and pickup points.

CAMPERS/MOBILE HOMES

With Guided Services—Expensive. Renting campers and mobile homes in Anchorage is expensive. Demand for them is high during the summer season and sources for renting them are limited. And don't forget the cost of hiring a guide to help you navigate the rivers. If time permits, driving your own camper to Alaska will help solve the cost problem, but be prepared to join many others who have the same idea and crowd the limited roads and campsites.

With No Guided Services—Moderate. Same comments as the guided camp system, but plan on do-it-yourself river or lake fishing. Obtain advice and detailed maps from fishing supply stores in the region. Also, Alaska state parks and fishing agencies are good sources of information.

TOWN LODGING

Local Inns with Guiding—Low. This is an interesting option if you are on a very limited budget. The idea is to get to a small town and stay at a local inn or bed and breakfast. Use the services of a local guide throughout your trip. The guide provides a boat or other transportation to fishing waters. The drawback is that you are limited to the regional waters.

REMOTE CABINS

Privately Owned Cabins, Non-Guided—Low. These cabins are situated close to waters in remote sites. Access is by float plane to lakes or adjacent rivers. This type of lodging requires bringing your own supplies, food and fishing equipment. Many

cabins are furnished and equipped with stoves and heaters. Requires that you have the outdoor skills to guide yourself.

Government Owned Cabins, Non-Guided—Very Low. These cabins have a minimum of facilities and equipment other than a stove and cots. Staying here requires that you bring all your food, supplies, bedding, and equipment. You must also have outdoor skills so you can guide yourself. Contact government parks and forest service agencies for details.

This overview of the lodging available, and the general price ranges, should help you select your preferred accommodations. Appendix 2 lists a variety of lodging at various prices.

HOW TO SAVE MONEY ON
RODS AND REELS

For the past four years, I have broken a fly rod at least once per Alaskan visit, sometimes more. But there are some good news and some lessons to be learned in breaking expensive rods.

On your first trip to a long-distance destination to catch big fish, you don't need to buy a large amount of expensive equipment. For king salmon, an effective fly fishing system is a Number 11 rod and quality reel with an excellent drag system. The first time you go to Alaska, I recommend you save money by borrowing rods and reels from the lodge or the guide. If you join me on one of my trips, you are welcome to borrow from me.

For a subsequent trip, after you are familiar with the gear

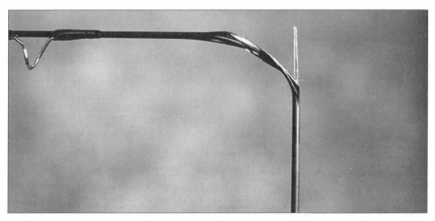

you need to catch Alaska's big fish, purchase a quality system that is correctly sized for the species you seek. Be certain the fishing rod supplier is an established firm that offers long-term warranties. Many manufacturers provide an unconditional lifetime warranty with guaranteed replacement and no questions asked. This type of warranty is the best.

Some suppliers replace broken rods very quickly. A few take as little as one or two weeks for replacement. If you go on many trips and use a common size rod, a fast replacement policy is very important. Check the supplier's track record for speed of replacement.

Optimum single rod	Number 7, good for up to 15-pound sockeye, chum and silver salmon; or Number 5, good for up to 10-pound trout and other native fish.
Optimum two rods	Numbers 8 and 5, also good for chum and silver salmon.
Optimum three rods	Numbers 11, 8 and 5, good for up to large kings and down to small arctic graylings.
Optimum four rods	Numbers 11, 8, 6 and 4, good match to all species expected in Alaska's fresh water. Provides overlap in the event of a broken rod.

If you are going to Alaska for salmon, take the largest fly rods that you would use in the lower 48 states. The table on page 114 shows optional sets to take on your trip. All are 9 or 9.5 feet in length.

Rods made in four or three pieces are compact and can be easily hand-carried on board the airplane for minimum damage.

If you are buying equipment for the first time and expect to spend a significant amount of money, you can try and negotiate a quantity discount for multiple items. If you do not get a reasonable offer, ask other stores or suppliers. Plan ahead. Ask your supplier if they have sales periods and when they occur. Try to negotiate prices based on sale prices and buying in quantity.

BUILD YOUR OWN ROD

One way to save on the cost of rods is to build your own from blanks. The initial cost for materials, tools and a short course on rod building will cover the cost of a new finished rod. As you build up a larger inventory of rods, your savings will increase.

Save Money Through Proper Maintenance

Another way to save money on rods is to properly use and maintain them.

1. Graphite rods are vulnerable to scratches. Avoid even small nicks and scratches that weaken the outer fibers of graphite composite rods by using cloth bags to cover them. Use carrying cases where possible, even in boats.

2. Don't place or transport rods against metal or other abrasive surfaces.

3. Take extra care when stringing rods. Thread

a loop of line through the guides, then pull the line through without bending the rod.

4. Weighted flies hitting rods cause damage to graphite. Use an open casting stroke, especially with sinking lines or sink tip lines.

5. Do not exceed a maximum bend of 90 degrees on rods. With fish on, use side-to-side motions with the rod as the fish comes close to you.

6. Snagged flies should be broken off by pulling on the line, with the rod tip pointing toward the snag. Don't use the rod to break snags.

7. Periodically wax the ferrules with paraffin.

8. Take rods apart when you have finished fishing to avoid stuck ferrules.

9. Before storing rods in tubes, completely dry them. Use dry rod cases for transporting in boats or planes.

10. To protect rod tips, bag them with tips and cork handles up. This way, the bottom impact loads are on the stronger ferrule tips.

11. Keep rods clean. Occasionally wash them with mild soap and warm water.

12. Use furniture polish to shine and protect rods.

Take good care of your rods and they will last a long time, saving you money.

SAVING ON REELS

In the long run it pays off to put money into a well-designed reel.

It costs less to buy one good quality, all-around reel that is suitable for most fish species in Alaska, than to buy several lower quality reels. A reel that will hold a Number 6 or 7 line plus 200 yards of 20-pound backing is adequate for all species.

There is one possible exception to a single reel approach. If you are going for big king salmon, a Number 10 through 12 line and 30-pound backing would be a better match. But, you can reduce your expenses by borrowing this equipment if you are going to Alaska for the first time after kings.

You might say a Number 7 line is overkill for catching a 1-pound grayling, but it is more humane to quickly bring in the fish, retrieve it and return it quickly to the water. The delay caused by playing the fish a long time with a very lightweight system, although it may seem more sporting and challenging, causes stress to the fish and is less desirable.

So what are the design requirements for a desirable reel for Alaska? One of the most important features is that the design be extremely simple, making the reel easy to disassemble, clean and reassemble. There are no parts stores in Alaska for quality reels and you must rely on your reel's inherent simplicity and ruggedness to be able to survive the sometimes harsh environment, temperature ranges, and dirt and sand particles that can easily foul it up.

The fewer pieces you have when you disassemble the reel, the better. Will one screw be all that you need to remove to take apart the reel for cleaning? Or are there many screws and small parts that will need to be carefully reassembled? What if you drop a critical part in the water—what is your backup plan? Think about these things before buying a reel.

I once saw, on the Alagnak River, a client who disassembled a very expensive but complicated reel to clean out some sand in the bearings. The reel was nearly impossible to reassemble because the client forgot the assembly sequence of all the parts of the reel. Even the experienced guide could not reassemble

it. A good test is to disassemble a reel in the store; if you cannot reassemble it yourself after an explanation, it is too complicated.

The design of the drag system is key. A large surface for the drag plate means a longer effective operation with heavy drag on when fighting big fish. Using the palm only for drag is not effective when a 30-pound fish takes off downstream.

A single reel that holds a floating line, plus another reel or backup spool holding a sink tip line, is all that is needed for most Alaskan fish, whether salmon or natives. An alternative to a backup spool is to use removable sink tip sets having quick disconnect loops at each end of the line and sink tip.

Protect the reel by using a reel cover whenever you are in transit between fishing holes or traveling up or down the river. Keep the drag off when traveling to retain the spring strength of the drag brake.

Chapter

11

HOW TO SAVE MONEY ON FLIES

It took me many years before I learned how to save money on flies for long trips to Alaska, Argentina or New Zealand. But once I learned, I saved a whole bundle.

It is difficult to resist the temptation to bring all the flies in all the sizes recommended by the standard fly list put out by lodges. The key to saving money is to focus on the flies most likely to be successful at the time of your fishing trip.

Some ideas for saving money on flies are as follows:

Obtain From Guide. Ask the lodge owner or guide to supply flies. Negotiate a package that flies are to be part of the trip, gratis. Or ask the guide to provide flies at no added cost. Most guides tie their own flies on their own time and keep a large supply at hand. And guides expect tips for the trip, so providing flies is not unreasonable as part of their service.

Buy in Quantity. If you do not tie flies, buy by the bulk. You will go through 10 to 15 flies a day, so buying the preferred fly in quantity will help save money.

Tie Your Own. Alaskan flies are large, very simple and much easier to tie than flies for streams in the lower 48 states. The raw materials are cheap. For example, if you plan on taking 300 flies for a week's trip, the retail price will run about $1000. But by tying your own, large savings are achieved, about one-tenth the amount or less.

Many fly fishing clubs throughout the country offer classes on fly tying. If your club does not, inquire at other clubs. Fly fishing stores frequently teach fly tying. There are several books on the topic that start with basic principles and use photos to illustrate each step along the way.

A local guide may offer to teach fly tying. Although I took courses at a club and at a store, my best experiences were in having guides personally show me while in Alaska.

The following example is illustrative of the savings gained by tying your own flies: The Bunny Fly is effective for catching many species of salmon. The Bunny Fly is made from rabbit fur, dyed to the desired color. One whole rabbit skin costs about seven dollars. Each skin yields about 200 flies, equivalent to less than four cents per fly. Add the cost of a few pennies for a hook, and you are talking about very low cost flies compared to $2.50 or more per fly at a retail shop. Reuse your hooks and you will really go cheap. You can even share the expense of fly tying supplies with a friend.

There is nothing as personally rewarding as tying your own fly, then watching it work in action, even if it is large and simple. The finale is the ultimate reward—a closeup photo of a big fish, caught with your hand-made fly in its mouth. I feel this same reward when I take Alaskan fish photos for my seminars (see Chapter 17 on how to take interesting photos of your flies and fish).

THE GETTING-READY-TO-GO STAGE:
PACKING LUGGAGE FOR ALASKA

On my first trip to Alaska in the early 1980's, I brought along insufficient equipment, the wrong size rods, improper flies and the wrong luggage. Subsequent trips included too many bags and unused or underused equipment. Finally, after my fourth or fifth trip, I brought along enough equipment and the correct luggage. I had found the proper balance between bringing enough equipment to be useful, but not too much to be heavy and cumbersome.

Following is my recommended luggage and equipment list for fly fishing trips to Alaska, when the objective is to catch all five species of heavy salmon and all native fish, including the small graylings. This list assumes you will stay at remote lodges, full-service camps or bed and breakfast accommodations with towels, linens and laundry services available for washing soiled clothing. Self-guided or self-equipped trips would require more equipment and different gear for outdoor living. All luggage should be soft- sided duffel type bags because they fit easily within the confines of float planes.

Also, I am assuming that local owners and guides will provide additional equipment that is not normally used, such as special flies for early or late run species of fish and special rods for larger than expected fish.

TRAVEL DAY

In order to be ready for fishing on arrival at my first destination, I dress at the start of air travel for fishing (except waders), even if I am staying overnight in Anchorage before the next flight to a camp. The reason I do this is so I am ready to fish, and I don't waste time and energy unpacking, redressing and repacking for a one-night stay in a stopover city. Dressing before the flight also helps in the event that checked-in baggage becomes lost in transit.

I usually change into the following clothes for fishing:

✧ Cotton heavy-duty pants, jean or denim, medium/dark color

✧ Mosquito-resistant canvas shirt, medium/dark color

✧ Heavy boots and light socks

✧ Light, waterproof jacket

✧ Broad-brimmed hat

✧ Ear plugs for use on noisy commuter aircraft
to final river

If you have multi-piece travel rods, always handcarry the rod case and tackle bag onto the plane. Check in the large duffel bag. Bring traveler's checks and cash for tips, and carry credit cards for larger purchases in the city or for car rental.

Carry Rod Case and Several Rods

Try to carry your rod case. Rough handling by baggage handlers can damage fly rods, causing scratches and nicks. Also, you run the risk of the airline losing your rods if they are checked, which would ruin your fishing trip.

If your objective is to catch all the available species of Alaskan fish, carry four rods: Numbers 4, 6, 8, and 11 weight. Rods with either three or four pieces are convenient and will fit, inside their rod carriers, into the overhead compartment.

Most regional aircraft in Alaska have no overhead baggage storage space, so be prepared to hand your rods to the ground crew, but keep your eyes on how they handle them. Use a rugged travel case for rods. I once saw a light aluminum tube case bent and folded due to being placed under heavy boxes in transit. Another time, a regional airline put the rods in a cloth bag without a case and the guides were bent flat.

If you are focusing on a particular specie, tailor the rods you bring to that fish. (See Chapter 10 on species and equipment.) If you are going on a multipurpose trip and you plan to do more

sightseeing than fish-
ing, reduce the num-
ber of rods and bring
only Numbers 7 and
11 for all-around fish-
ing. These rods will
work for small
graylings to large king
salmon. Another alter-
native if bringing a
minimum number of
rods is to bring a
Number 8 and 5 com-
bination, or a Number
7 and 5 pair, then bor-
row the house rods for
larger king salmon.

If you are planning
to hike or camp and
need very lightweight equipment, bring only a four-piece Number
7 rod in a short tube tied to your backpack. This rod is effective
for catching most Alaskan fish, both salmon and native.

Carry Tackle Bag or Backpack

Handcarry aboard the airplane a tackle bag containing the
essentials for minimum fishing, just in case the checked-in
bags get lost or their arrival at the remote camp is delayed.
Include the following:

✓ Most important reels (best reels for most
desirable fish)

✓ Most important flies (best flies for desirable fish)

✓ Essential medicines

✓ Insect repellent (regional airports have many mosquitoes)

✓ Pocket tissues

✓ Sunblock lotion

✓ Lip balm

✓ Polaroid glasses

✓ Toiletry bag (for overnight use in Anchorage)

✓ Camera in Zip-lock plastic bag

✓ Extra camera lenses in Zip-lock plastic bags

✓ Film in Zip-lock plastic bag (or in X-ray film protector bag)

✓ Airline tickets

✓ Car rental certificates, if applicable

✓ Cash for tips

✓ Traveler's checks

✓ Notebook and pencil for diary of photos and fish caught

✓ Itinerary

✓ Alarm clock

✓ First aid kit

✓ Small flashlight

Depending on your destination, it may be essential to bring bottled water. Do not drink any stream or lake water in Alaska unless it is treated. The lodge or guide should have all other fishing essentials available until any lost baggage is retrieved.

Check In Large Duffel Bag

Pack everything else in a single large duffel bag to be checked in at the home airport. The reason for the single bag is that if you plan to bring salmon home, you will probably check in a box of fresh fish on the return flight that weighs up to 50 pounds or more. The airline limit is two checked-in bags without an extra charge. I have been caught on the return flight with two luggage bags and one fish box, and ended up paying for one extra bag all the way back home. It is very expensive.

In the large duffel bag include the following for a one-week trip:

✓ Remainder of reels

✓ Remainder of fly boxes

✓ Fishing vest (I prefer a vest with a built-in life preserver)

✓ Rainproof jacket (good quality if you can afford it)

✓ Fleece jacket

✓ Rainproof pants

✓ Three canvas shirts, medium or dark colors

✓ Two denim or jean pants, medium or dark colors

✓ Two pairs of lightweight thermal underwear

✓ Undershorts

✓ Pajamas, if desired

✓ Extra gloves, including fleece or neoprene for cold weather

✓ Socks

✓ Baseball cap

✓ Wool cap, for cold weather

✓ Extra medicines

✓ Extra tissues

✓ Chest-high waders

- ✓ Wader belt

- ✓ Felt-bottom boots

- ✓ Towel

- ✓ Plastic bags, for wet boots and soiled clothes

- ✓ Knife

- ✓ Motion sickness pills if ocean fishing

Include the following in the vest:

- ✓ Nippers

- ✓ Hemostat

- ✓ Scissors,

- ✓ Assorted split shots No. 4 and No. 6

- ✓ Fly floatant,

- ✓ 10- and 15-pound leader for salmon,

- ✓ Leaders or tippets, 4–10 pound, 2x to 5x, for char, trout and grayling

- ✓ Sink tips with end loops for quick disconnect to fly line

- ✓ Hook sharpener

- ✓ Fisherman's tape, for protecting blisters or sensitive fingers

- ✓ Strike indicators

✓ Water thermometer (optional)

Twice I have nearly drowned when fast currents and loose gravel caused my footing to loosen and my body went with the current. Buoyancy is important when wading and a buoyant upper body is essential in the water to compensate for the buoyant lower body when wearing waders. Fortunately, I am a fairly competent swimmer. But I now use a vest with a built-in safety float system, and I don't care what other people think of my vest appearance. When it comes to lifesaving safety measures I err on the safe side.

Note that all airlines have size and weight limits for checked bags. At the time of this writing, on most domestic airlines, you can check two pieces of baggage for free, subject to weight and size limits.

There are also size and weight limits for carry-on bags. Carry-on bags must fit under the seat or be stowed in an approved compartment or overhead bin. Check the fine print that accompanies your airline ticket. It specifies weight and quantity limits for checked and carry-on bags. If not specified, contact your airline for the rules and avoid extra baggage fees or having your carry-on denied because it is too heavy or too large.

Fly Tying Bag (Optional)

A difficult decision is whether or not to bring a fly tying bag. The answer lies mainly in whether the destination lodge maintains proper tying equipment and supplies.

Even if a lodge states that fly tying equipment is available, the supplies for the fly for a specific fish may be out of stock, simply because they were used up by others at the lodge before your arrival. Confirm the availability of fly tying materials for the days of your visit.

If you tie flies, keep the tying bag well stocked for almost any circumstance in the region. Just before your departure confirm with the lodge whether all supplies are available.

Regardless, try to identify the 10 most useful flies for the region when you go, prepare them and bring them. Then rely on the lodge's fly tying bench and lodge supplies to fill in the gaps.

OVERNIGHT IN ANCHORAGE

When going to any remote lodging in Southcentral or Southwest Alaska from the lower 48 states, it is almost impossible to get to your destination on the same day. This means that an overnight stay in Anchorage is unavoidable.

But in your pursuit of an affordable trip, paying very high in-season prices for an overnight stay in Anchorage is not very desirable. If you are accustomed to first-class hotels in big cities, the downtown hotels and luxury accommodations near the airport may be to your liking. If you are on a limited budget, though, saving on a one-night stay en route is desirable. The fol-

lowing list gives lodgings in Anchorage in all price ranges. For a more complete list with descriptions, see Appendix 5.

DOWNTOWN FIRST-CLASS HOTELS

Hotel Captain Cook. In the heart of downtown; easy walk to Cook Inlet Bay and the train station; no airport van; expensive.

Hilton Hotel. Near many downtown shops; walk to train station; no airport van; expensive.

Sheraton Hotel. Slightly removed from heart ofdowntown; no airport van; moderate to expensive.

Westmark Hotel. Two-hundred rooms in downtown Anchorage at 5th Ave and G Street; walking distance to train station and downtown stores and restaurants; no airport van; moderate to expensive.

MOTELS AND INNS

Copper Whale Inn. Restored historic home; downtown; moderate.

Comfort Inn. Downtown near Ship Creek; moderate.

Day's Inn. Near downtown; coffee shop; moderate.

LODGING NEAR AIRPORT

Best Western Barratt Inn. Large motel with restaurant; near airport; airport transportation; moderate.

Regal Alaskan. Luxury hotel on lake at airport; airport transportation; expensive.

Spenard Motor Hotel. Economy lodging on Spenard Road; near Alaskan style restaurant and McDonald's; free shuttle from and to airport; freezer for fish; inexpensive. Ask for John.

SIGHTSEEING IN ANCHORAGE AREA

While you are in the Anchorage area, these activities may be of interest to you.

Downtown walking tour—Drive or take a taxi to the Visitor Information Center, a log cabin with sod and grass on the roof in the center of the city. Then walk a few blocks to the railroad station (near the Hilton), which is an original Alaska Railroad System terminal, and see its display of an original steam locomotive.

If you have some time, take a train to Denali Park, stay

overnight (see Appendix 5), visit the park and return the next day. Or take a bus tour to Valdez and stay overnight, then take a boat cruise past glaciers on the return to Portage, ride on a short railroad through a tunnel, and return by bus to Anchorage.

Another option is to take a one- or two-day trip to a remote lodge, like the Talaview Resorts or Great Alaska Fish Camp (see Appendix 4). Transportation is provided, so you don't have to rent a car.

A completely different fishing experience is to travel down the Kenai peninsula to Homer or Seward and halibut fish in the ocean at Cook Inlet or Prince William Sound. It requires at least a two-night stay to rent an all-day halibut fishing boat (see Appendix 5). Fresh halibut is one of the most delicious ocean fish available in Alaska.

Chapter

14

THE IMPLEMENTATION STAGE:
FLY FISHING TECHNIQUES
FOR ALASKA

Now that you have a plan for going to Alaska, here are some
fly fishing pointers you should know based on some of my own
experiences. They should help you to fly fish more effectively
once you get there.

One of the nice things about fly fishing in Alaska is that
there are no special techniques or casting skills required other
than those learned to fly fish anywhere else. For example, most
of the fish are caught using a dead-drift technique. In some
cases, accuracy is called for, just like in the lower 48 states,

where placing a dry fly within a few inches above a protective cover helps. Having sink tip lines helps, since some fish stay near the bottom, while others vary in depth.

ARCTIC CHAR

My first arctic char was caught on the Kamishak River near Lake Iliamna. During the previous night, the guide suggested I tie up some Glo-Bug flies. This was during my early days of fly tying and I proceeded to use a very large hook, a 1/0 saltwater type bait hook with a large gape. I made a nice, large ball from champagne pink wool, almost one-half inch in diameter.

When the guide saw it the next morning, he said it was too big, the wrong color and not likely to work. I proceeded to use it on the Kamishak River. On my first cast, I dropped the fly well away from the main stream, about one-half the distance from the main flow to the shore. I saw a very large char come swimming quickly from its holding position in the center channel and travel about 15 feet to my fly. Then the char instantly scooped up the fly and swam away for its life. Because of its unfortunate mistake, and to my happiness, we had a fresh six-pound char for shore lunch. As a result, I have named that Champagne Glo-Bug, Sam's Ugly Number 2. (Number 1 is described below.)

Arctic chars are effectively caught from late May until October, but the peak periods are in June and September or October. The technique is to cast across the stream above the holding chars and let the fly dead-drift until the line is nearly straight downstream. Then strip in the line in quick, jerky motions. Try an assortment of flies, including alternate egg patterns, fish flies and nymphs.

ARCTIC GRAYLING

My first grayling was caught on the Kijik River just north of Lake Iliamna on the Bristol Bay drainage. It was heavily overcast that day, so the fly-out pilot decided not to go to a regular river that was obscured by the clouds. Rather, he proceeded to a lake that flowed out on the Kijik River. After parking the plane, the pilot, the guide, my associate and myself proceeded down the river starting from the lake outlet. It seemed we walked for many miles, not seeing any grayling. The guide was going by gut feel, since he was not as familiar with this river as he was the primary river that we could not reach.

As we were searching for the grayling, we came across hundreds of sockeye salmon, on their way upstream to spawn. It was sometimes so dense that I stepped on some and the salmon scattered like scared jackrabbits. Regardless, the objective was not salmon, but the grayling that should have been waiting below each group of salmon for eggs to be laid.

After some six hours of hiking downriver, we were about to give up when the guide did the right thing, which he should have done much earlier in the day. He went scouting ahead of the party much further downstream. Then he yelled back to us that he had found them.

I tried a medium cream-colored Caddis fly placed about 10-feet upstream of the holding grayling. On the first cast, one grayling came up from the pool about six-feet below and attacked the Caddis like it was dinner after fasting for days. A very rewarding 18-inch grayling, with a beautiful turquoise spotted large dorsal fin, was the result, and I have included that fish and fly in my slide shows. Subsequent grayling on that trip were taken with Royal Wulffs, Gold Ribbed Hare's Ears and Pheasant Tails.

We were so absorbed in the fun of catching grayling that we forgot to look at our watches. The base camp got worried and started to send a chase plane for us, thinking we were in distress. All's well that ended well, though, and we had a fine time for the day.

Arctic grayling are caught from May to October when they leave their winter holding positions in large rivers and go upstream to salmon spawning areas. The peak times for grayling are in late May, early June, then again in September and October.

Keep casting to grayling in front of deep holes, simulating dry flies that fall into the river in the riffles just above the hole, so the fly appears as if it fell in upstream. Similarly, get the nymphs down to the bottom well before the pools. Use 7-foot leaders for nymphs and 12-foot for dry flies.

CHUM SALMON

My earliest chum salmon fishing was on the rivers flowing near Lake Iliamna. But the most interesting and satisfying chum fly fishing I have experienced, was on the Alagnak near the outlet into Bristol Bay. I was at a lodge in the lower river and had just tied some Fuchsia Bunny Flies after dinner. Fishing with a guide was officially over for the day (typically an eight-hour fishing day), but there was plenty of light remaining because darkness falls near midnight in Alaska in July. So I talked a guide into taking me out in a boat, then letting me off the boat after reaching a hole about 500 yards from the lodge. I asked that he come get me a few hours later.

I proceeded to fish alone using the Fuchsia Bunny Fly (Chapter 6). After a few quarter casts, a 10-pound chum took the fly and ran away like a horse on a racetrack. Chum's don't do cartwheel somersaults like many other fish, but they have tremendous power to pull the line out. My hand was struck and beaten by the spinning handle of the reel as the fish pulled

away quickly. It takes a strong drag system on the reel to keep the fish from running away. After 15 minutes of tiring pulls, the chum finally gave in and was easy to land, the Fuchsia Fly still firmly imbedded in its mouth.

Chums are caught between the end of June and October. But the peak is in July and August. Chums like to hold and travel in groups. Cast over a wide arc repeatedly and wait until the first bite when the school passes by. Then quickly cast over the same spot. Experiment with different depths, because the vertical location is not predictable; chums cruise at different heights. Try a variety of strips, short and fast as well as long and slow. Then use the one that works best.

KING SALMON

Kings are worthy of their name. They are the largest of the salmon family to enter into Alaskan waters, averaging 35 to 40 pounds and can be as much as 50 pounds or more. The odds are that someone in a group in a lodge during a one-week stay at a premier river will land a king above 50 pounds, a real trophy.

My most interesting experience fishing for kings was with a borrowed rod. It was a house rod belonging to the lodge owner. It was 10-weight with a system called the Cheater, a large 3/0 salt-water hook with a white wool tail tied at the eye. Just above the hook was a large Styrofoam ball about the size of a golf ball, painted in Day-Glo red-orange. The entire system was weighted down with a heavy sinker located about two feet above the hook on a 15-pound leader. It was hardly a system worthy of being called a fly by purists of the sport, but it worked very well.

I was drifting the Cheater along the river about 15 feet from shore, sweeping an area known for cruising kings migrating upstream. Suddenly the king took the fly and ran off rapidly downstream, the current helping it to speed off. The reel on the borrowed rod was a level-wind gear reel and I made the mistake of not setting the drag, letting it free spool. The result when the fish took off was the worst backlash I have ever experienced. It took almost 30 minutes to clean up the mess on the spool.

I assumed the fish took off and was clear of the fly. As I was reeling the cleared line back on to the spool, I felt a slight tug on the line. The king was still on the line, waiting below the boat for me to finish clearing the reel and start the fight all over again. The fish never let go of the fly in all that time. It turned out to be a 40-pound male king. During that week, we brought in and released 15 to 20 kings per boat per day. The rate doubled for the number of fish we hooked but lost. You can see that Alagnak is one of the best rivers in Alaska for kings.

There are three regions on any river for king fishing: tidal waters or estuaries, and mid-river and upriver spawning areas. In tidal waters and mid-river locations, it is difficult to sight fish for kings, so a search and find method using power boats is the most effective technique. Float trips are a somewhat difficult way to catch kings because the float cannot repeatedly power to position over a hole. Upriver, many locations can be effectively sight fished for kings.

No one knows why kings go after gaudy, colorful flies. One plausible answer is that it is an irritant when such flies are presented in front of their noses during a run toward spawning. So they aggressively snap at the irritant. At least that would be the plausible answer if humans were similarly interrupted during mating. The kings in the summer, like all salmon, are not feeding and it does little good simulating other fish that they eat in the ocean.

So take a bright, gaudy fly like the Chartreuse Everglow fly or a Flash fly and present it as close to the king's nose as possible. How do you find the nose when the water is cloudy and deep? The answer is through trial and error. Keep casting to various locations in the resting pools or drift over likely runs of kings going upriver along the banks.

If casting to kings, use quarter casts, dead-drift the fly and retrieve in long strips. The point is to get the fish tired before attempting to bring it close to the boat, otherwise, with its strength, it will easily break off the leader or a knot. And finally, take a closeup photo of your large king with a fly in its mouth. The limit on the number of kings that can be caught, as of 1996, is one fresh king per day and two fish per season. All other kings are returned to spawn to provide others with an equal opportunity for a fish worthy of the title, the King of Alaskan Rivers.

PINK SALMON

The pink salmon arrive in abundance in Alaskan rivers during June through August, with the peak a few weeks during July. They predominately come to rivers to spawn during even years, 1996, 1998, 2000, etc. Pinks are relatively small in the salmon family, averaging about six pounds.

The males are larger than the females. They develop a large hump on their back as they prepare for spawning; therefore, they are sometimes referred to as the humpy. They do not travel far upstream like other salmon, so they can be located in abundance near the outlet of rivers to the ocean, mostly in tidal waters where they spawn.

The best technique is to dead-drift in holding areas—pools or eddies in the river. An alternative is to find calm water near tidal waters during peak high tide or peak low tide. Retrieve by stripping the line in short bursts. Don't be surprised if you foul hook several times with the highly dense population in the peak periods.

SILVER SALMON

On my first trip to Alaska many years ago, I took my wife, her sister and my mother-in-law and went to the Kenai River. It was September and the morning chill was uncomfortable, but bearable. We were awakened at 5:00 a.m. with fresh coffee and juices and, after a quick breakfast, were on our way upstream to the guide's favorite fishing hole. We got there about 6:30 a.m. The wind was very calm, the pools were glassy smooth and no sound or motions disturbed the early morning scene.

We dropped Coho streamers into the pool and started to retrieve in short quick strips. The ladies were grumbling about having to wake up so early, having to take potty breaks in the grass, freezing their fannies in the cold and thinking it would have been better to have stayed in a warm bed.

Then, suddenly in the quiet still air, pandemonium broke loose when my mother-in-law hooked into a large 13-pound silver salmon. It flew into the air, did somersaults, went back down deep, came up again to do wheelies, down again, up again. It was an unbelievable display of acrobatics from a huge silver.

After landing the fish, we took photos of mom holding her prized possession. It was the biggest silver of the trip and a memorable event for her. She would go back to Alaska at the drop of a hat, and she continually joined us for our forays into New Zealand, where she again set a group record for enjoyable

fly fishing, regardless of age.

So the best technique, after finding a pool where silvers are likely to be holding for rest, is to cast just upstream and make short strips fairly fast. If there is no bite, then vary the stripping speed and length of strip, six inches to two feet, both slow and fast. Vary the sinker or sink tip weights to vary the depth of the fly.

Silver salmon come up from the ocean during July to October, with their peak months being August and September. If you enjoy sight fishing for salmon, stay with clear nonglacial waters. Dress warmly against the cold morning air, as the wind chill from traveling on high speed boats and the cool weather in Alaska in late summer and early fall, can make you feel uncomfortable.

If the river is very clear and it is a sunny day, switch to darker patterns. If it is cloudy or overcast, stay with bright colors. If streamers do not work, switch to appropriately colored Woolly Buggers, sizes 2 to 4.

SOCKEYE SALMON

During one of my earliest trips to Alaska, I went to the Alagnak River. The guide stopped the boat at a strange point in the river, a narrow spot where there was a fast running main channel and still waters on the shallow sides. Sockeyes were migrating upstream along the shallows where the water was slower and calm.

As the salmon passed through this area, they traveled in groups of about 10 fish. They formed a V-shaped pattern as they swam upriver. The lead fish was the pathfinder and all other sockeyes followed, creating this V pattern. I could not see

the fish coming, but I clearly saw the wake of the group creating the V on the surface.

I tied on a Sockeye Orange fly, which is very simple and sparse, with tinsel wrapped around the shank of the hook and a few wraps of orange hackle behind the eye. I cast it across the river, timing it so that during the retrieve, the fly passed the pathfinder fish. Using short bursts of stripping, the fly imitated an object that was getting in the way of the path of the swimming sockeyes.

The situation is like two cars arriving at the same intersection, one being at a right angle to the other, on a collision course. The fly presents an irritating and potential threat to the sockeye moving upstream. Sockeyes will snap at the fly and frequently will spits them out, but there is a chance that it will be hooked in the mouth. At other times, it is easy to foul hook on the body. To assure this collision course, the depth of the fly presentation is critical. If the fly passes over the fish or under, it does no good and adjustments to weight or speed of retrieval are needed.

Sockeyes arrive in June through August and are seen in abundance in holding waters or as they reach spawning grounds. The colors, especially on the males, are fascinating as they prepare for mating. The body turns a deep red and the head a dark green. The males develop a dominant hooked mouth.

The best technique is to use four-foot leaders, 10-pound strength, and a light sink tip or some lead that just submerges the fly to the depth of the sockeyes. This weighting is critical, because the sockeye will not move vertically to take a bite at the fly. Cast slightly forward and across the holding or traversing fish. Strip in short bursts in an aggressive manner toward the fish.

RAINBOW TROUT

I have fished for rainbow trout all over Alaska, but one of the most memorable occasions was on the Kenai River several years ago. The Kenai is glacial water with a milky turquoise color, so there is no sight fishing there. The rainbows were found throughout the river, but mainly in areas where salmon were congregating to spawn.

A young guide was showing me around in a two-person drift boat, stopping at likely holes in the river as we drifted downstream. We passed the Russian River intersection with the Kenai, where there are hundreds of fisherpeople congregated five-feet apart in an area called the Combat Zone.

Proceeding downstream, we stopped at a hole in a channel to the side of the main river to prepare our flies. The guide showed me a technique on real-time fly tying, without a vise, in the middle of the river. Take a good size hook, about a 1/0 salt-water bait hook, tie a Snell knot on the shank and let the leader pass through the eye. By forcing the leader back a short distance into the eye, a loop is created in the leader.

He then took a large plastic box, like a saltwater fly box, with holes drilled into the top of each compartment. In each compartment was a different colored ball of yarn.

The guide looked around, felt the temperature of the water and based on his judgment, picked a color to create his instant fly. He took a short section of yarn, cut about a one-inch section, then passed it through the loop in the leader. After he cinched down the loop, the yarn was trapped in the leader and a very rough looking wing was created coming out of the sides of the hook.

He then asked me to pick a color. I chose three: red, apricot and white. I cut them to length, inserted all three into the loop and cinched down on the leader. The guide looked at the instant fly and said it was ugly, the wrong colors. I proceeded to fish with it.

In the next hole, I had a few nibbles from small rainbows testing the fly, but no real strikes. Then a strong pull by an obviously large fish kept me busy for about 15 minutes. But I could not see the fish because the water was milky and opaque. After I successfully brought in the rainbow, it turned out to be a very pretty, leopard skin-patterned rainbow 26-inches long and weighing about six pounds.

The unwritten code of ethics in Alaska at that time was that one rainbow can be kept for mounting if the length is at least a trophy class, 24 inches or more. So I kept the fish and had it mounted. It remains in my den as a reminder of the best time I had on the Kenai.

But I experienced a sad ending to this trip the next day. I liked the process of tying instant flies and catching fish on the spot so much that I tried the same river and location again. The same three-colored fly and technique were used. This time I hooked and brought in a whopper, a 33-inch rainbow trout on a fly, almost a yard long. This was just two inches below the known record for the Kenai River.

But the rules are that only one trophy rainbow per trip is a keeper, so it was too late to mount the 33-inch fish. Back into the river it went for the next person to try and get.

In my seminars on demonstrating how to tie Alaskan flies, I use this fly as an example of how simple Alaskan flies can be and yet have such effectiveness against the native fish. I have named this three-colored fly Sam's Ugly Number 1. (And please be careful how you pronounce this name. It is not "Sam is Ugly Number 1.")

Rainbows are caught over a long season, but the peak months are in June, September and October. The late season rainbows are generally heavier and fatter than the early rainbows because they binge on salmon eggs all summer.

The early trout are caught by using flies that simulate young salmon (smolts) going out to sea, so a simulated smolt pattern and size is appropriate. Late season rainbows can be caught by simulating the eggs and the flesh that comes off of the carcass of adult salmon after they finish their spawning. A Ginger Bunny Leech is an effective flesh fly during the late season. Another alternative is a White Woolly Bugger.

Use of Glo Bug or Iliamna Pinkie flies with weights are effective and can be cast just below the salmon redd (nesting) area to pick up several waiting rainbows. Use sink tip lines with a four- to six-foot leader. An alternative is to use a floating line, a 12-foot leader and indicators to show the fish taking the wet fly.

Chapter

15

Bears in Alaska

The following is a guideline from the Alaskan Department of Fish and Game on how to handle encounters with bears.

Bears are curious, intelligent and potentially dangerous animals, but undue fear of bears can endanger both bears and people. Many bears are killed each year by people who are afraid of them. Respecting bears and learning how to properly behave in their territory will help both you and any bear you might encounter avoid needless suffering. Bears tend to avoid people. In most cases, if you give a bear the opportunity to do the right thing, it will.

BEARS DON'T LIKE SURPRISES!

If you are hiking through bear country, make your presence known, especially where the terrain or vegetation make it hard to see. Make noise, sing, talk loudly or tie a bell to your pack. If possible, travel with a group. Groups are noisier and easier for bears to detect. Avoid thick brush. If you can, try to walk with the wind at your back so your scent will warn bears of your presence. Contrary to popular belief, bears can see almost as well as people, but trust their noses much more than their eyes or ears. Always let bears know you are there.

Bears, like humans, use trails and roads. Don't set up camp close to a trail they might use. Detour around areas where you see or smell carcasses of fish or animals, or see scavengers congregated. A bear's food may be there and if the bear is nearby, it may defend the cache aggressively.

DON'T CROWD BEARS!

Give bears plenty of room. Some bears are more tolerant than others, but every bear has a "personal space"—the distance within which a bear feels threatened. If you stray within that zone, a bear may react aggressively. When photographing bears, use long lenses; getting close for a great shot could put you inside the danger zone.

BEARS ARE ALWAYS LOOKING FOR SOMETHING TO EAT!

Bears have only about six months to build up fat reserves for their long winter hibernation. Don't let them learn human food or garbage is an easy meal. It is both foolish and illegal to feed bears, either on purpose or by leaving food or garbage that attracts them.

Cook away from your tent. Store all food away from your campsite. Hang food out of reach of bears if possible. If no trees are available, store your food in airtight or specially designed bear-proof containers. Remember, pets and their food may also attract bears.

Keep a clean camp. Wash your dishes. Avoid smelly food like bacon and smoked fish. Keep food smells off your clothing. Burn garbage completely in a hot fire and pack out the remains. Food and garbage are equally attractive to a bear so treat them with equal care. Burying garbage is a waste of time. Bears have keen noses and are great diggers.

If a bear approaches while you are fishing, stop fishing. If you have a fish on your line, don't let it splash. If that is not possible, cut your line. If a bear learns it can obtain fish just by approaching fishermen, it will return for more.

CLOSE ENCOUNTERS: WHAT TO DO.

If you see a bear, avoid it if you can. Give the bear every opportunity to avoid you. If you do encounter a bear at close distance, remain calm. Attacks are rare. Chances are, you are not in danger. Most bears are interested only in protecting food, cubs or their "personal space." Once the threat is removed, they will move on. Remember the information in the following paragraphs:

Identify yourself.

Let the bear know you are human. Talk to the bear in a normal voice. Wave your arms. Help the bear recognize you. If a

bear cannot tell what you are, it may come closer or stand on its hind legs to get a better look or smell. A standing bear is usually curious, not threatening. You may try to back away slowly diagonally, but if the bear follows, stop and hold your ground.

Don't run.

You can't outrun a bear. They have been clocked at speeds up to 35 mph, and like dogs, they will chase fleeing animals. Bears often make bluff charges, sometimes to within 10 feet of their adversary, without making contact. Continue waving your arms and talking to the bear. If the bear gets too close, raise your voice and be more aggressive. Bang pots and pans. Use noisemakers. Never imitate bear sounds or make a high-pitched squeal.

If attacked.

If a bear actually makes contact, surrender! Fall to the ground and play dead. Lie flat on your stomach, or curl up in a ball with your hands behind your neck. Typically, a bear will break off its attack once it feels the threat has been eliminated. Remain motionless for as long as possible. If you move, and the bear sees or hears you, it may return and renew its attack. In rare instances, particularly with black bears, an attacking bear may perceive a person as food. If the bear continues biting you long after you assume a defensive posture, it likely is a predatory attack. Fight back vigorously.

In most cases, bears are not a threat, but they do deserve your respect and attention. When traveling in bear country, keep alert and enjoy the opportunity to see these magnificent animals in their natural habitat.

Chapter

16

PRECAUTIONS—
MOSQUITOES, HYPOTHERMIA
AND WATER SAFETY

Alaska can be hostile and harmful if precautions are not taken against the harsh environment. Three dominant concerns should be addressed when exposed to the Alaskan outdoors.

MOSQUITOES

Welcome to the land of the mosquito, also known as the Alaskan state bird. And mosquitos aren't the only biting insects that hunger for exposed human skin, there are also the White Sox. They are big and appear in huge numbers during the peak summer months when salmon come to spawn. The

itching from only one bite will last a long time.

I learned a lesson many years ago on the Kenai River when I went on a drift boat and was eaten alive. I had taken no insect repellent on the boat and had no way of powering back to a source of repellents. After suffering many bites, another boat finally came near and I gratefully obtained a dose of the protective lotion. Never again will I venture into the Alaskan wilds without carrying or wearing adequate protection.

There have been many technology developments since the old days of wearing bulky nets over one's exposed skin. Four new methods that have been developed to combat these pests are improved netting, improved lotions, proper clothing, and room and tent aerators.

New netting products are now available that maintain a separation between the skin and the outer screen barrier. These are more effective than the old style of single layer nets, which are vulnerable at points where the net touches the skin and no protection is available.

Improved lotion products are proving to be more effective. At the time of this writing, however, there is a controversy on the use of lotions that contain DEET. Recently, there was a case reported about a fatality allegedly related to use of a product containing DEET. The reader is cautioned to be aware of the contents of such products, to obtain expert advice concerning the use of such products and, if appropriate, to consider use of alternative lotions. A new product introduced in 1996 claims to be an insect repellant, sunscreen and lotion all-in-one liquid, without the use of DEET.

Proper clothing is the most practical solution for protecting most body surfaces. Clothing made from dense canvas, like the material used for awnings, is effective. Shirts and pants made from this canvas will deter many of the biting insects. A simple approach to packing is to take only outer clothing made from canvas. That way, you won't forget and wear non-canvas clothes during the trip. A slight disadvantage to this approach is that, on hot days (not likely in Alaska), canvas shirts can be uncomfortable. But discomfort is less important than avoiding getting nasty bites from huge Alaskan mosquitoes.

There is another product that is useful to prepare bedrooms and tents for the night. It is an incense product available at most stores in Alaskan towns, which is effective in driving out mosquitoes from closed areas. Use it before retiring.

A final note—none of these measures protect in special situations when the skin is exposed, such as going to the bathroom in the wide open spaces. When nature calls, try to avoid heavy brush and marsh areas and take care of your business quickly. Good luck.

HYPOTHERMIA

Hypothermia is substantially lowered body temperature due to the loss of body heat. It results because the body is not able to replace the heat loss caused by being subjected to cold temperatures, especially in cold water.

It is the major cause of death in boating accidents. Often the cause of death is listed as drowning, but most often the primary cause is hypothermia and the secondary cause is drowning. After individuals have succumbed to hypothermia, they will lose consciousness and then drown. The following chart shows the effects of hypothermia:

Water Temperature, Degrees Fahrenheit	Exhaustion or Unconsciousness
32.5	Under 15 minutes
32.5 to 40	15 to 30 minutes
40 to 50	30 to 60 minutes
50 to 60	1 to 2 hours
60 to 70	2 to 7 hours

Hypothermia can also result from exposure to cold air, cold wind and cold wet air. Inadequate insulation and protection from the elements also aggravates hypothermia.

If you are exposed to cold and wet conditions, immediately get out of your wet clothing and into dry clothes to provide warmth and protect yourself from further chilling.

SAFETY IN THE WILD AND WATER

Wilderness survival requires training and experience. Make certain that at least one person in your party, but preferably all, have had formal training in survival in the wild. This type of experience is critical.

In most parts of the Alaskan wilderness, medical assistance

is nearly impossible to obtain. First aid training and cardiopulmonary resuscitation (CPR) training are essential for at least a member of the party, and preferably all members.

To stay safe in the water:

1. Stay with a competent, experienced guide at all times. - Let the guide know about your skills in swimming, or lack thereof.

2. To minimize exposure to deep or unsafe waters, learn to cast long distances. For example, use the double haul cast or Spey rods when working wide rivers.

3. Never go deeper than you can recover if you slip. This might be knee deep for people with poor swimming ability or hip deep for others who have adequate swimming skills.

4. Use a vest with a built-in flotation system. When you fall into the river and the water is above your head, the waders are more buoyant than the upper body with a heavy equipped vest. The head, therefore, naturally sinks while the feet tend to float. You want the reverse, head up and feet down.

And most important, talk to the guide before venturing on trips. Tell the guide of your limitations in physical ability, both in swimming and general health. Make certain the guide understands that you are concerned about going into dangerous situations. Insist on safety or don't go in the water or into risky environments and situations.

Chapter

17

HOW TO TAKE INTERESTING PHOTOS WHEN FLY FISHING

After a trip, are you disappointed when your photos turn out to be less than you expected? Do your photos show small people and small fish? Are the faces and the fish in shadows and not readily visible? Most of these problems stem from the fact that the human eye and mind compensates for poor lighting and images while the camera does not. As a result, you get less than professional photos.

Here are a few simple rules on taking outstanding photos when outdoors. For taking photos of fish and flies, some additional pointers are recommended.

> 1. Load film in camera properly. A lesson to learn the hard way is to not feed the film properly, then to find that, when you thought the film was at the end, the film had never moved in the camera.

> 2. Get close to the subject. Completely fill the frame with the subject. If the person holding the fish is the subject, move close enough to fill the frame. If the fish is the subject, get close enough to capture most of the fish.

3. If you want a photo of scenery with a person in the foreground, take two shots. Have the person stand to the side and get a total landscape shot. Then get a closeup of the person with part of the landscape in view.

4. Take a good closeup of the fish's head with a fly in the mouth. Use a macro lens to get really close to flies and the fish's mouth. Open the mouth, get really close and show how the fly was hooked.

5. Use flash at all times, day or night. That way, the shadows are filled in with light. If the person in the photo is wearing a hat, their face will appear hidden without fill-in flash. The fish may also appear dark if there is any cloud cover or the sun is behind the subject being photographed.

6. Quickly revive the fish. If photos take too

much time, first revive the fish by moving the fish in the water until strength returns. Then quickly take more photos. A professional photo group once took a trophy trout and revived it 10 times, taking over 100 photos of the same fish, before finally releasing it safely.

7. Try different photos to remind you of the visit. Take a photo of the meals; most of the food is good, even in tent camps. Include the chef holding a favorite dish!

8. This is a trip of a lifetime—a happy trip—so smile, smile, smile !

Chapter
18

HOW TO BE A GOOD GUEST

This topic was suggested by a lodge owner and, thinking of my own experiences, it makes a lot of sense. I have visited many lodges and have taken many guided trips with groups. There are occasions when a visitor makes life very difficult or miserable for the lodge owner or other guests. I believe all readers who take trips have experienced this problem.

In Alaska, the situation is aggravated by being in a remote site. The problems are often primarily caused by the very high expectations of the guest, which cannot be fulfilled because

there are no remedies available.

I don't intend to lecture, but some common sense solutions are noteworthy so everyone can have a good time. To enjoy fishing and the total outdoor experience, be understanding. Understand that you are in the wilderness, in the middle of nowhere.

Fishing is not 100 percent perfect all the time. Fish arrive at different times each year. Although it is somewhat predictable, the exact date may vary by several weeks from year-to-year. Lodge owners and guides try to be ready for contingencies and find alternate rivers or species if the primary water and fish did not arrive when you did. If the fish turns out smaller or fewer than normal, it may be unusual, but it happens. What happens one year can be quite different from the next year.

The staff at a lodge cannot control the weather. If it is extremely windy, fly casting can be difficult or impossible, but a skilled guide can compensate by teaching alternate methods, such as roll casting with the wind. If it rains every day of the trip, which can happen, no one has any ability to change it.

The environment is totally different than an urban office situation. There are no rigid timetables of appointments, schedules to meet and places to be at specific times. Relax, go with the flow and be flexible. This is your vacation and less formal timing of events is part of the scene.

Be patient and be courteous to others. If you have a legitimate complaint or concern, voice it to the appropriate staff or management who can take action. But don't take it out on others or hold it inside and let it build up steam.

In the end, it helps to thank the staff for trying, even if events were uncontrollable and the trip turns out to be less than expected. In summary, be understanding.

Appendix

1

FISH SPECIES AND FLIES

Although my experience tells me that most Alaskan fish will take a few flies better than others, there are times when using a variety or different patterns from the norm is very effective. The following are suggested flies from which to select a variety of alternative flies.

In any event, it is highly recommended that you contact the destination owner or guide within a month of your arrival to find out if any unusual patterns or types of flies would work best on a given date. For clear water, use smaller and darker flies. For murky water, use brighter, larger flies.

Fish the fly along the bottoms of rivers with a long broadside drift. In deep or swift runs, cast slightly up-and-across stream, mend several times, then let it hang and swim in the current for several minutes. For salmon, use weighted flies attached to 3- or 4-foot level leaders of 10- to 12-pound test Maxima (green); use 15- or 20-pound test in deep, fast flowing heavy runs.

For flesh flies, present the fly straight downstream in the vicinity of the salmon carcass. Use a weighted fly; add additional No. 4 or No. 5 split shot to the leader at the eye of the fly until the fly swims close to the bottom. Swim the fly several minutes in the vicinity of the carcass, moving it slowly back and forth across the current with the rod tip, occasionally letting a few pulls of line play out freely to simulate a chunk of salmon flesh floating away.

To fish salmon egg patterns, use a 7 or 8 weight, 9-foot or longer rod, a floating line, a long leader, split shot on tippet or pinched onto a short drop a foot from the fly in shallow water. Get the fly in front of the fish's nose.

ARCTIC GRAYLING
Adams, size 10–18
AP Black Nymph, size 8–18, weighted
Black Gnat, size 4–10
Blue Winged Olive, size 14–18.
Bunny Bugs, size 8–12, bright colors
Elk Hair Caddis, size 4–10
Flash Body Nymph, size 8–14, pearl Mylar body over red
Gold Ribbed Hare's Ear Nymph, size 8–14
Glo Bugs, size 8–12, champagne pink
Katmai Slider, size 2–6
Light Cahill, size 10–20
Mosquito, size 14–20
Royal Wulff, size 10–18
Woolly Bugger, size 8–2, dark colors

CHUM SALMON (ALL FLIES WEIGHTED)
Alaskabou, size 4–8
Bunny Bugs, size 4–6, yellow, chartreuse, fuchsia, white
Chartreuse Bunny Fly, size 1/0–6
Coho Streamer, size 4–6, green/white, red/white, yellow
Egg Sucking Leech, sizes 2 and 4, brightly colored
Flash Flies, sizes 2 and 4, brightly colored
Fuchsia Bunny Fly, size 1/0–6
Popsicle, size 4–8
Sparkle Shrimp, sizes 2 and 4, chartreuse, hot pink, orange

KING SALMON
Bunny Bugs, size 2, yellow, chartreuse, pink, fuchsia, white
Coho Streamers, size 2, green/white, red/white, solid yellow
Egg Sucking Leeches, sizes 1/0, 2, and 4, bright colored
Everglow, sizes 3/0, 1/0, 2, and 4, chartreuse, pink, orange
Flash flies, sizes 1/0, 2, and 4, bright colored
Sparkle Shrimp, size 1/0–6. hot pink, orange
Whistler, size 3/0, black and orange, light blue
Wiggletail, sizes 1/0, 2, and 4. chartreuse, pink and orange
Woolly Buggers and Bunny Flies, size 1/0–4, pink, orange

Pink (Humpy) Salmon (all flies weighted)
Bunny Bugs, size 4–6, yellow, chartreuse, fuchsia, white
Coho Streamer, size 4-6, green/white, red/white, solid yellow
Egg Sucking Leech, sizes 2 and 4, bright colored
Flash Flies, sizes 2 and 4, bright colored
Fuchsia Bunny Fly, size 8
Polar Shrimp, size 6–10, orange
Single &Double Egg, size 6–10, matching salmon egg color

RAINBOW TROUT, DOLLY VARDEN AND ARCTIC CHAR

AP Black Nymph, size 10–18
Babine Special, size 2–6
Battle Creek Special, size 2–8
Blue Smolt, size 4
Coronation, two-egg sperm fly, size 2–8
Deer Hair Mouse, size 1/0 –2
Egg Sucking Leech, size 2–4
Egg Sucking Sculpin, size 1–4
Flashabou Nymph, size 10–18
Ginger Bunny Leech, size 2–8
Glo Bug, size 6–10, light pink, light orange, dark orange.
Gold Ribbed Hare's Ear, size 8–16
Humpy, size 4–18, all black
Iliamna Pinkie, size 6–8, light pink, light and dark orange
Kauffman Stonefly Nymph, size 6–2
Little Black Stonefly Nymph, size 10
Lime Colored Stonefly Nymph, size 10–12
Marabou Nymph, size 10–18
Matuka Streamer, size 2–4, olive or black
Mickey Finn, size 2–10, silver body, yellow over red over yellow
Olive Woolhead Sculpin, size 8–12
Parachute Adams, size 10–18
Pheasant Tail Nymph, size 8–16
Rio Grande Trude, size 8–14, black body, white wing
Royal Coachman, size 10–18
Sam's Ugly No. 1, size 1/0–6
Sam's Ugly No. 2, size 6–8

Simple Shrew, size 2
Sparkle Shrimp, size 6–10, hot pink
Woolly Bugger, size 8–12, purple, black, chartreuse body, black hackle and tail (also brown, olive)
Zug Bug, sizes 8 and 10

SILVER (COHO) SALMON (ALL FLIES WEIGHTED)

Babine Special, size 6–8
Bosses, size 6–8
Bunny Bugs, size 4–6, yellow, chartreuse, fuchsia, white
Coho Streamers, size 4–6, green/white, red/white, yellow
Eggsucking Leech, size 4–8, bright colored
Everglow Fly, size 4, chartreuse, orange and white
Flash Fly, size 1–3, bright colored
Fuchsia Bunny Fly, size 1/0–6,
Purple Woolly Bugger, size 4–8

Sparkle Shrimp, size 4, cerise, chartreuse, and fluorescent

SOCKEYE (RED) SALMON

Gold Comet, size 6–10, gold tinsel on body, ginger hackle.
Montana Brassie, size 6–10, copper wire body, white wing.
Sockeye Orange, size 6–10. mostly size 8, sparsely tied
Sockeye Chartreuse, size 6–10, sparsely tied
Sockeye Purple, size 6–10, sparsely tied

A p p e n d i x

2

Lodging, Campgrounds and Guides

The lodges and guide services listed here are close to waters that I believe provide high-quality, productive fishing. Your actual results may be highly dependent upon timing, circumstances and other conditions that are variable from year to year.

This is not a complete list of Alaskan lodging for quality fishing. Although I have attempted to characterize the lodging and services based on my knowledge and referrals by others, the reader is reminded of the disclaimer statement at the front of this book.

If you do contact any of the lodges or guide services listed, I would appreciate your giving my name as your source. Giving my name as a referral helps me to improve my database. Also, please let me know any

Extremely Expensive	$6000 and above
Very Expensive	$5000 - 6000
Expensive	$4000 - 5000
Moderate Cost	$2500 - 4000
Low Cost	$1500 - 2500
Very Low Cost	Under $1500

updated information you discover about the lodge or guide service.

The following are approximate price ranges for lodging in Alaska. At the time of this writing, summer 1996, the costs are roughly as shown. All costs are per week, in U.S. dollars; all food, lodging and guiding is included unless specified otherwise. Airfare to Alaska is additional unless specified otherwise.

Alagnak Lodge. On Alagnak River—full-service guided lodge - located at premium location on Alagnak River - excellent fly fishing for chum salmon in front of lodge, premium king salmon downriver within 5 to 10 minutes by boat - long distance from rainbow areas up river - floatplane from commercial airport at king salmon is included in price - dedicated and hardworking staff - lodge can be crowded - dining and recreation in same room, all guests and staff in same two-story structure - moderate cost.

Owner: Vin Roccanova   P. O. Box 351
4117 Hillcrest Way   King Salmon, AK 99613
Sacramento, CA 95821   (907) 439-5001 (Summer)
(800) 877-9903 (Winter)

Alaska Adventures. Guided float trips in Bristol Bay areas and Togiak National Wildlife Refuge - specializing in remote areas - limited party size for each trip - group or individual bookings - spin or fly fishing.

Owner: Chuck Miknich
P. O. Box 111309
Anchorage, AK 99511
(907) 345-4597

Alaska Dream Lodge. Full-service guided lodge - specializes in Aniak River, Kuskokwim River, Wildlife Refuge - moderate to expensive.

Owner: Larry Jarrett   Route 1
Alaska Dream Lodge   Kuna, ID 83634
P. O. Box 143   (208) 922-5648 (winter)
Aniak, AK 99557
(907) 675-4304 (summer)

Alaska Fishing Adventures. Guides on Tikchik, Nuyakuk, Nushagak and Goodnews Rivers - float trips and tent camp.

Owner: Barry Johnson
1334 Bannister Drive
Anchorage, AK 99508
(907) 278-9607

Alaska Fishing with Terry Adlam. Fly-in fishing camp on the Mulchatna River - comfortable camp, hot showers - guide for every two people.

Owner: Terry Adlam
P. O. Box 670597
Chugiak, AK 99567
(907) 696-1575

Alaska Freshwater Safaris. Float trips in Bristol Bay and Kodiak areas.

Owner: Roger Denny
P. O. Box 770752
Eagle River, AK 99577
(800) 688-1032

Alaska Gulf Coast Adventures Inc. Guided tent camp - outstanding service - provides fly-outs - pickup and return to Cordova airport included in price - famous for large silver salmon in fall - can have more inclement weather than Bristol Bay - low to moderate cost. (See Appendix 4).

Camp Kiklukh
Owner: George Davis
Manager Pat Pendergast

P. O. Box 1849
Cordova, AK 99574
(800) 950-5133

Alaska National Forest Cabins. For information and reservations, contact:

U.S. Forest Service
Information Center
  Centennial Hall
  101 Egan Drive
  Juneau, AK 99801
  (907) 586-8751

Alaska Rainbow Float Adventures. Complete seven-day float trips on Alagnak River - fly fish.

Owner: Ron Hayes
P. O. Box 39
King Salmon, AK 99613
(800) 451-6198

Alaska Rainbow Lodge. Located on Kvichak River, 15 miles below outlet from Lake Iliamna - commercial flights to King Salmon, then lodge floatplane to lodge - premium rainbow fishing on Kvichak in fall - full-service lodge with daily guided fly-outs to all five species of salmon - fishing right on Kvichak River in event of inclement weather - flightseeing included - full-service lodge and comfortable accommodations - separate lounge and elegant dining room - private bathrooms - expensive. (See Appendix 4.)

Owner: Ron Hayes
P. O. Box 39
King Salmon, AK 99613
(800) 451-6198

Alaska River Adventures. Float trips on rivers in Bristol Bay area - features naturalist floats and small groups - started in 1978.

Owner: George Heim   (907) 595-1422
P. O. Box 725   (800) 595-8687
Mile 48.,2 Sterling Highway, Suite P   Fax (907) 595-1533
Cooper Landing, AK 99572

Alaska State Parks. For campground information, contact:

Alaska Public Lands Information Center
605 West Fourth Avenue, Suite 105
Anchorage, AK 99501 - 5162
(907) 271-2737

Alaska Vacation Planner (free). A summary catalog listing selected lodging, local transportation, tours and visitor's highlights - focused on sightseeing and tourist visitors. For copies, contact:

Alaska Division of Tourism
P. O. Box E
Juneau, AK 99811-0800
(907) 465-2010

Alaska Wilderness Expeditions. Specializes in float trips down three rivers: Talachulitna River, American Creek and Mulchatna River - pick up and drop off in Anchorage, includes one night in Anchorage hotel - bring your own bedding and tackle - some outdoor experience and floating skills helpful - guests-to-guide ratio varies from 5 to 1 to 8 to 1, depending on river - guests provide help in camp operations - prices low to moderate.

Owner/Guide: Tim White
Alaska Wilderness Expeditions
2508 Strasburg Road
East Fallowfield, PA 19320-4228
(610) 380-0103

Alaska Wilderness Outfitting Company. Float trips and equipment rentals.

Alaska Wilderness Outfitting Company
P. O. Box 1516
Cordova, AK 99574
(907) 424-5552

Alaska Trophy Fishing Safaris. Private fishing camp with river boats, motors, and tent camp offering guided service on Mulchatna River.

Owner: Dennis Harms
P. O. Box 670071
Chugiak, AK 99567
(907) 696-2484

Alaska Wilderness Expeditions. Provides guided and outfitted river float trip on Talachulitna, Chilikadrot and Mulchatna Rivers - complete package - space limited to minimum of three and maximum of seven per trip.

Owner: Tim White   (215) 380-0103 (winter)
Box 237   Rd 5   (907) 333-2662 (summer)
Coatesville, PA 19320

Alaska Wildwater. For equipment rental information, contact:

Alaska Wildwater
P. O. Box 110615
Anchorage, AK 99511
(907) 344-8005

Alaska's Wilderness Lodge. Full-service, daily fly-out lodge on Lake Clark - fly-outs to Bristol Bay, Lake Iliamna, Lake Clark and Katmai Park areas - limited home waters fishing - capacity 24 guests - expensive.

Tim Cudney   (907) 272-9903
P. O. Box 190146
Anchorage, AK 99519

Anchor River Inn. Lodging at Anchor River on Kenai Peninsula.
Anchor River Inn
P. O. Box 154
Anchor Point, AK 99556
(907) 235-8531

Angler's Alibi Tent Camp. Outstanding kings, sockeyes, chums right in front of camp using Fuchsia Bunny Fly - full- service tent camp with limited fly-out to excellent rainbow and char fishing in Katmai Park - outstanding personal service - very good food - limited to nine guests - showers in bathhouse - separate outhouses - moderate cost - a real value. (See Appendix 4.)

Owner: Karl Storath   (607) 869-9397
6105 Poplar Beach   Fax (607) 869-9656
Romulus, NY 14541

Aniak River Lodge. Located on Kuskokwim and Aniak River junction, in Aniak, Alaska - outstanding salmon and northern pike with fly fishing equipment during season - new lodge, just finished in winter of 1996 - long distance from Anchorage, but excellent value - must be certain salmon are running - low to moderate cost. (See Appendix 4.)

Owner: Lee Brooks
P. O. Box 29138
Bellingham, WA 98228-1138
(800) 747-8403 (September through May)

Ayakulik Camp. Guide service and lodging on Kodiak Island.
Ayakulik Camp
P. O. Box 670071
Chugiak, AK 99567
(907) 696-2484

Beaver Creek B & B. Continental breakfast, cable TV,exercise equipment, sauna, phones, fax, private entrance, fully equipped kitchen.

Owners: Susan and Gordon Isaacs   (907) 842-1231 (days)
P. O. Box 563   (907) 842-5366
Dillingham, AK 99576

Bergie's Guide Service. Daily guided or drop-off fishing on Kanektok River and Southwestern Alaska - overnight accommodations with kitchen facilities.

Owner: Bruce Bergman   P. O. Box 2295
P. O. Box 151   Bethel, AK 99559
Quinhagak, AK 99655   (907) 543-4148 (winter)
(907) 556—8347 (summer)

Bill Martin's Fish Alaska, Inc. Lodged-based fishing on Yantarni Bay.

Owner: Bill Martin   (907) 346-2595 (winter)
Bill Martin's Fish Alaska, Inc.   (907) 842-2725 (summer)
P. O. Box 1887   (907) 563-6384 (alternate)
Anchorage, AK 99510

Blue Heron Inn in Yakutat. Lodging in town of Yacutat, easy access to river - guide service - focus on two runs of steelhead trout, ranging from 8 to 20 pounds; fall run starts in late August and continues through winter; spring run begins early March, peak around first of May, finish by end of June - low cost.

John Latham
Blue Heron Inn
P.O. Box 254
Yakutat, AK 99689
(907) 784-3287

Blue Mountain Lodge. Full-service lodge with daily fly-out -

located on Becharof Ugashik Lake region - also big game guiding - photography - and flight-seeing tours.

Owner: Tracy Vrem   (907) 688-2419
P. O. Box 670130   Fax (907) 688-0491
Chugiak, AK 99567

Branch River Lodge. Full-service lodge on Alagnak River - low to moderate prices.

Owner: Bob DeVito, Jr.   P. O. Box 513
9508 N. E. 180th   King Salmon, AK 99613
Bothell, WA 98011   (206) 486-5316
(206) 486-5316 (winter)

Brightwater Alaska. Wilderness float trips throughout Bristol Bay, Alagnak, Goodnews, Kisarolik, Nushagak, Mulchatna and Koktuli Rivers and Naknek Lake system.

Owner: Chuck Ash   (907) 344-1340
P.O. Box 110796   (907) 344-4614
Anchorage, AK 99511

Bristol Bay Charter Adventures. Operates 10-passenger catamaran with tours and transportation on Naknek River into Katmai National Park, Brooks Camp - lodging consists of two wilderness cabins with sauna and kitchenettes - boat rentals.

Owners: Patrick & Diedre O'Neill P. O. Box 185
P. O. Box 4281   King Salmon, AK 99613
Soldotna, AK 99669   (907) 246-3750 (summer)
(907) 262-2750 (winter)

Bristol Bay Lodge. Full-service lodge, capacity 24 guests - home water on Lake Agulowak - daily fly-outs using 3 Beavers - wilderness overnight tent camping in Wood River, Tikchik area, then back to lodge and to another tent camp - expensive.

Owner: Ron McMillan
2422 Hunter Road
Ellensburg, WA 98926
(509) 964-2094 (winter)

Box 1509
Dillingham, AK 99576
(907) 842-2212 (summer)

Bristol Bay Rafters. Equipment rental for unguided float trips in Bristol Bay area - canoes, rafts, kayaks and camping equipment available - will assist in planning, organizing trip.

Owner: Jim Nagel
P. O. Box 841
Dillingham, AK 99576
(907) 842-2212

Brooks Lodge. Lodge located in Katmai National Park - adjacent to famous Brooks Falls where brown bears feed on leaping sockeye salmon - fishing, hiking, programs by park service rangers - noted for fishing for rainbows, arctic graylings, lake trout and sockeyes (in season) - buffet dining three times daily - main lodge has spectacular view of Naknek Lake - cocktails for purchase - bus tours to scenic extinct volcano area - maximum 60 guests in 16 units - fly from Anchorage to King Salmon on commercial plane (cost not included in package) - open early June to mid-September - contact Katmailand, Inc. for further information.

Katmailand Inc.
4550 Aircraft Drive
Anchorage, AK 99502
(800) 544-0551

Chugach National Forest. For information on cabin rentals, contact:

Chugach National Forest
201 East Ninth Avenue, Suite 206
Anchorage, AK 99501
(907) 271-2500

Copper River Lodge. Unique - a fly fishing only lodge on the Copper River flowing into Lake Iliamna - catch and release - sockeye during July - log cabin lodge - jet boats to access river - guided - no fly-outs.

Owners: Dennis and Sharon McCracken
P. O. Box PVY   P. O. Box 200831
Iliamna, AK 99606   Anchorage, AK 99520
(907) 571-1464 (summer)   (907) 345-9022 (winter)

Crystal Creek Lodge. High-quality full-service lodge located 25 miles northwest of Dillingham on Lake Nunavaugaluk - daily guided fly-outs using float plane or helicopter - expensive.

Owners: Terry Eberle and Dan Michels
P. O. Box 3049
Dillingham, AK 99576
(800) 525-3153

Kusack's Alaska Lodge. Full-service lodge with daily fly-outs and float trips to all Bristol Bay region - hunting and photography - expensive.

Owners: Robert and Lula Cusack   8920 S. E. 45th Street
P. O. Box 194   Mercer Island, WA 98040
Iliamna, AK 99606   (206) 232-3278 (winter)
(907) 571-1202 phone and fax (summer) Fax (206) 232-1029

Dave Duncan and Sons. Fuided fishing on Kanektok River - float trips.

Owner: Dave Duncan
High Valley Ranch
Route 1, Box 740
Ellensburg, WA 98926
(509) 962-1060

Diamond Lodge: Located on Naknek River - unguided fishing - access via King Salmon airport.

Owners: Heidi and Johann Wolf   P. O. Box 497
Weimarer Strasse 17   King Salmon, AK 99613
35759 Driedorf, Germany   (907) 246-3011 (summer)
Overseas phone 011-49-2775-7711 (winter)

Deep Creek Fishing Club. Scenic location just south of Kasilof River on Kenai Peninsula on bluffs overlooking river and Cook Inlet Bay - close to large kings, other salmon and halibut - distant from upper river rainbows - full-service lodge covering Kenai, Kasilof, Ninilchik, Deep Creek and nearby rivers - moderate prices.

Deep Creek Fishing Club
P. O. Box 410
Ninilchik, AK 99639
(800) 770-7373

Eruk's Wilderness Tours. Float trips for small groups to Alagnak, Aniak, Chilikadrotna, Kodiak, Nushagak, and Salmon Rivers - tents provided - includes commercial flights from Anchorage - low to moderate prices.

Eruk Williamson
Eruk's Wilderness Tours
12720 Lupine Road
Anchorage, AK 99516
Phone/Fax (907) 345-7678

Fishing Unlimited Lodge. Two deluxe lodges on Lake Clark, just North of Lake Iliamna, with daily fly-out trips to entire Bristol Bay area up to 250 miles radius - float trips - use of river boats - maximum 16 guests - four guests per floatplane/pilot/guide - cabins house one to three guests - bathrooms in cabins - hot tubs and saunas - includes flight from Anchorage - expensive to very expensive.

Owner: Lorane Owsichek
P. O. Box 190301
Anchorage, AK 99519
(907) 243-5899 (winter)
Fax (907) 243-2473 (winter)

General Delivery
Port Alsworth, AK 99653
(907) 781-2213 (summer)
Fax (907) 781-2244 (summer)

Fox Bay Lodge. Guided fishing full-service lodge with daily fly-outs - located on Naknek River, 7 miles east of King Salmon - expensive.

Owner: Klaus Steigler
P. O. Box 13
King Salmon, AK 99613
phone and fax (907) 246-6234

Freshwater Adventures, Inc. Floatplane access in Bristol Bay area.

Freshwater Adventures, Inc.
P. O. Box 62
Dillingham, AK 99576

(907) 243-7676 (winter)
(907) 842-5060 (summer)

Glacier Bear Lodge. Full-service lodge and guide service in Yakutat - private baths in rooms - on-site restaurant and lounge.

Glacier Bear Lodge
P. O. Box 303
Yakutat, AK 99689
(907) 784-3202

Goodnews River Lodge. Deluxe tent accommodations located on Goodnews River - full service - jetboat fishing and float trips.

Owner: Ron Hyde
4909 Rollins
Anchorage, AK 99508
(907) 333-2860
Fax (907) 338-5356

Great Alaska Fish Camp. Quality full-service lodge with daily guide service and optional fly-outs available - separate cabins with

bedrooms and toilet and shower in each room - main lodge has two lounges, dining - guides to Upper and Lower Kenai River - check lodge for days river is open for salmon fishing from boats - low to moderate prices. (See Appendix 4.)

Manager: Lawrence John
HCI Box 218
Sterling, AK 99672
1-800-544-2261, Fax (206) 638-1582

Grosvenor Lodge. Access to rainbows, chars, lake trout, and sockeye salmon (in late July and early August) right in front of lodge - full-service lodge within Katmai Park, but no fly-outs - all access to waters by jetboat - accommodations limited to maximum of six guests - three guest cabins, modern bathhouse away from cabin - dining, lounge, kitchen in main lodge with view of Grosvenor Lake - complimentary cocktails - price includes round-trip from Anchorage, equipment and waders if needed - low to moderate prices.

Katmailand Inc.
4550 Aircraft Drive
Anchorage, AK 99502
(800) 544-0551

Iguigig Boarding House. Lodging, guided and unguided on Kvichak River, equipment and boat rental, airport pickup and dropoff - assist with float trips - freezer for salmon.

Owner: Dan Salmon   (907) 533-3219
P. O. Box 4003   Fax (907) 533-3217
Iguigig, AK 99613

Iguigig Lodge. At outlet of Iliamna Lake - full-service lodge - limited to eight guests - outstanding fall rainbows.

Larry and Elizabeth Todd
P.O. Box 871395-F
Wasilla, AK 99687
(907) 376-2859

Iliamna Airport Hotel. Referrals for transportation and guide services in Lake Iliamna area.

Iliamna Airport Hotel
P. O. Box 157,
Iliamna, AK 99606
(907) 571-1501.

Iliamna Bearfoot Adventures. Full-service lodge on Copper River (Southeast) - Lookout Mountain, Lake Iliamna - equipment rentals.

Owners: Greg and Sally Hamm   P. O. Box 1146
P. O. Box PVY   Willow, AK 99688
Iliamna, AK 99606   (907) 495-6388 (winter)
(907) 571-1477 (summer)   Fax (907) 563-1076

Iliaska Lodge. Uniquely fly fishing only, full-service lodge, located on Lake Iliamna - daily fly-outs, fishing Kodiak, Katmai and Iliamna area - also drive to Tazimina and Newhalen rivers - capacity 20 guests - expensive.

Ted Gerken
6160 Farpoint Dr.
Anchorage, AK 99507
(907) 337-9844

Kanektok River Safaris, Inc. Full-service tent camp on Kanektok River in Lower Kuskokwim area.

Owner: Joshua Cleveland
P. O. Box 9
Quinhagak, AK 99655
(907) 5560-8211, Fax (907) 556-8814

Karluk Lodge. Full-service lodge on Kodiak Island on Karluk River. - limited days for runs of salmon.

Kodiak Lodge
P. O. Box 3
Karluk, AK 99608
(907) 241-2229

Katmailand, Inc. Operators of key facilities within Katmai National Park and the Bristol Bay area, including Brooks Lodge - Kulik Lodge - Grosvenor Lodge, and several float trips with cabins in Bristol Bay area - operates bus and float plane trips to park; highlights include volcanoes and scenery - ask for Sonny.

Katmailand, Inc.
4550 Aircraft Drive
Anchorage AK, 99502
Telephone (800) 544-0551

Katmai Lodge. Very large lodge on Alagnak River, about half way between upper river "braids" for rainbows and graylings and lower river with salmon - separate lounge with fly tying table and dining room - plentiful food served cafeteria style - three guests assigned per guide - bunk style beds - flush toilets and showers at ends of buildings - caution: get a confirmed assignment to fly fishing teams, especially for kings, otherwise you may be dissatisfied.

Owner: Tony Sarp
Katmai Lodge

2825 - 90th S. E.. Dept. FM
Everett, WA 98208
(206) 337-0326

Katmai National Parks Campgrounds. For information, contact:

Katmai National Parks and Preserve
P. O. Box 7
King Salmon, AK 99615
(907) 486-2659

Kalsin Inn Ranch. Full-service lodging and guiding on
American River, Kodiak Island.

Kalsin Inn Ranch
P. O. Box 1696
Kodiak, AK 99615
(907) 486-2659

Kenai Lake Lodge. Rooms on Kenai Lake, Kenai Peninsula.

Kenai Lake Lodge
P. O. Box 828
Cooper Landing, AK 99572
(907) 595-1590

King Ko Inn in King Salmon. Full-service inn with restaurant
on premises - package with guiding available - low prices.

P. O. Box 346
King Salmon, AK 99613
(907) 246-3377

Kodiak National Wildlife Refuge. Kodiak Island cabins - contact:

Kodiak National Wildlife Refuge   (907) 487-2600
1390 Buskin River Road
Kodiak, AK 99615

Kodiak Adventures. Guide service on Kodiak Island.

Kodiak Adventures
P. O. Box 1403
Seward, AK 99664
(907) 373-2285

Kulik Lodge. Full-service luxury lodge within Katmai National Park with daily fly-outs - fish for rainbows in front of lodge - boat to adjacent Kulik Lake and Nonvianuk Lake - fly-outs within 100 miles of lodge provide access to kings, chums and silvers in addition to sockeyes and pinks - maximum capacity is 20 guests - two to a cabin with shower and bathroom - lodge with large fireplace, dining and bar with complimentary cocktails - price includes round-trip from Anchorage - expensive. Possible plan for 1997 - basic with no fly-outs, moderate cost. Optional fly-outs, expensive.

Optional late season with reduced price - end of September to mid-October - no fly-outs, focus on large rainbows. For information, call:

Katmailand, Inc.
4550 Aircraft Drive
Anchorage AK, 99502
(800) 544-0551

Mahay's Riverboat Service. Based in Talkeetna - provides daily upriver transportation on jetboats - stay in Talkeetna or float trips or camp upriver.

Mahay's Riverboat Service
P. O. Box 705
Talkeetna, AK 99676
(907) 733-2400

Mark Emery Guiding Services. Guides in King Salmon area on Naknek River - stay in King Salmon inns or B&B's.

Mark Emery Guiding Services   (904) 288-3341

P. O. Box 516
Ocklawaka, FL 32179

Mission Lodge. On Aleknagik River near Dillingham - full- service lodge with daily guided fly-outs to Bristol Bay area - home water is Wood River - capacity 30 guests - former missionary retreat - one bed per room, central washroom on third floor, private baths on second floor - fly fishing equipment provided - expensive to very expensive.

Dennis Gebhardt   (907) 349-2753
200 W. 34th St. Suite 1160   fax (907) 344-4594
Anchorage, AK 99503

Morrison Guide Service. Guides in King Salmon area on Naknek River - stay in King Salmon.

P. O. Box 161
King Salmon, AK 99613
(907) 246-3066

Nonvianuk Lake Cabins & Float trips. Very low prices. For information, contact:

Katmailand Inc.
4700 Aircraft Drive, #2
Anchorage, AK 99502
(800) 544-0551

No-See-Um Lodge. Full-service lodge on Kvichak River between Levelock and Igiugig - guided daily fly-outs throughout entire Bristol Bay area - capacity eight guests, two to a room - three float planes - fly fishing only - if weathered in, can fish local Kvichak river - expensive.

Jack Holman
6266 Riverside Dr.
Redding, CA 96001
(916) 241-6204

fax (916) 244-4618

Nushagak Outfitters. Guide services.

Owner: Randy Triplett
P. O. Box 734
Dillingham, AK   99576
(907) 344-4672

Ole Creek Lodge. Full-service guided fishing.

Ole Creek Lodge
506 Ketchikan Street
Fairbanks, AK 99701
(907) 452-2421

Ouzel Expeditions. Guided floatfishing.

Ouzel Expeditions
P. O. Box 935
Girdwood, AK 99587
(907) 783-3220

Paxson Lodge. Full-service lodge and guiding in Gulkana area

Paxson Lodge
P. O. Box 3001
Paxson, AK 99737
(907) 822-3330

Quinnat Landing Hotel. Modern hotel on Naknek River in King Salmon - created nine years ago by group of doctors in Anchorage - provides full-service packages including guides, transportation and all meals - trips to Katmai National Park - open all year, but no guiding in winter - ice fishing - in late March, features large steelheads, averaging 10 to 16 pounds - separate lounge and dining room - meals include steaks, Carabou, other items from menu - moderate prices.

Quinnat Landing Hotel   (907) 246-3000
P. O. Box 418   (800) 770-3474
King Salmon, AK   99613

Rainbow King Lodge. On Lake Iliamna - luxurious, large, full-service guided lodge with daily fly-outs - package includes sightseeing trips by air - excellent fishing in exclusive leased rivers - expensive. (See Appendix 4.)

General Manager: Craig Augustynovich
333 S. State Street, Suite 126
Lake Oswego, OR   97034
1-800-458-6539, Fax (503) 635-3079

Rainbow River Lodge. Direct access to Copper River (southeast region, flows into Lake Iliamna), large rainbows in late summer - no fly-out in basic program, limited to local waters - moderate prices - with optional daily fly-outs, expensive.

Chris Goll
Rainbow River Lodge
4127 Raspberry Road
Anchorage, AK   99502
(907) 243-7894

River Beauty B & B. Room and breakfast inn at Talkeetna - combined with local guiding service is a low-priced package.

River Beauty B&B
P. O. B ox 525
Talkeetna, AK 99676

Royal Coachman Lodge. Full-service lodge on Nuyakuk River in Wood, Tikchick Lakes region - daily fly-outs with capacity of 12 guests - expensive.

Bill Martin   (907) 346-2595
P. O. Box 1887
Anchorage, AK 99510

Ruffitters. Float trips on the Gulkana River.

Ruffitters
P. O. Box 397
Gakona, AK, 99586
(907) 822-3168

R.W.'s Fishing. Guides and two bedroom condos on Kenai Peninsula - provides all types of fishing, fly fishing and conventional - fly-out options - specializes in kings during May to July, sockeyes in mid-June through mid-August, silvers in August and September and halibut through mid-August in adjacent Cook Inlet - no meals, airfare or car rentals in price - low prices.

R.W.'s Fishing
P. O. Box 3824
Soldotna, AK 99669
(800) 478-6900

Saltery Lake Lodge. Full-service lodging on Kodiak Island.

Saltery Lake Lodge
1516 Larch Street, Suite One
Kodiak, AK 99615
1-800-770 5037

Talaview Resorts. Full-service, landscaped lodge on hill - excellent scenery, clear water and fly fishing action for salmon and rainbow - 40-minute air taxi transportation from Anchorage provided.

(See Appendix 4.)

Owners/Managers: Steve and Louise Johnson
P. O. Box 190088
Anchorage, AK 99519
Phone / Fax (907) 733-3447

Talkeetna Riverboat Service Guides. Guiding only on
Talkeetna river system.

Owner: Mac Stevens   Phone (907) 733-2281
P. O. Box 74
Talkeetna, AK 99676

***Tikchik Narrows
Lodge.***
  Full-service lodge with
daily fly-outs in Bristol
Bay and Kuskokwim
drainages - expensive.

Bud Hodson
(907) 243-8450
    P. O. Box 220248   Fax (907) 248-3091
    Anchorage, AK 99522

U. S. Geological Survey, Earth Science Information Center.
for topographic maps, contact:

USGS Earth Science Info. Center
4230 University Drive, Room 101,
Anchorage, AK 99508-4664

Valhalla Lodge (Alaska Safari, Inc.). Full-service lodge located
near Lake Clark - combination of fly-outs, river jet-boats, float trips,
covers waters from Bristol Bay ocean to Katmai Park and Iliamna
areas - fly-outs five days, local waters by boat two days including
Tazimina River - lodge holds 12 guests - two to a room - expensive.

Owner: Kirk D. Gay   (907) 243-6096
P. O. Box 190583
Anchorage, AK 99519-0583

Westmark Kodiak Hotel

236 Rezanof West,
Kodiak, AK 99615

Wood River Lodge. Tikchick Lake

Owners: John and Linda Ortman
P. O. Box 997
Whitefish, MT 59937

Appendix

3

AIRLINES AND AIR TAXIS IN ALASKA

The following airline offices and air taxi services may be of help to you in planning the use of regional and local airlines in Alaska. Regional and local airlines are essential to get to many rivers because of the lack of roads.

If you do make inquiries with any of these transportation services, I would appreciate your giving my name as your source. Using me as a referral helps me keep my information database current.

135 Air Taxi. To destinations in Bristol Bay area. Also provides guided and unguided fishing tours.

Gary Bishop
P. O. Box 3409
Palmer, AK 99645
Telephone (907) 745-7282

Affordable Car Rental Company. Reserve early for four-wheel drive vehicles.

4707 Spenard Road
Anchorage, AK 99517
(907) 243-3370

Alaska Helicopters. Helicopter taxi.

Alaska West Air, Inc. To destinations in Bristol Bay area, Lower Kuskokwim, all National Parks. Provides fly-in fishing, floating and sightseeing trips.

Doug Brewer
P. O. Box 8553
Nikiski, AK 99635
Telephone (907) 776-5147

Bay Air. To destinations in Dillingham. Fly-out fishing, drop off, floating and equipment rentals.

Tom Schlagel/Janet Armstrong
P. O. Box 714
Dillingham, AK 99576
Telephone (907) 842-2570, (907) 842-2470

Branch River Air Service. King Salmon based, covers Bristol Bay area. Guided and unguided fishing. Raft rental. Coordinates lodging. Access to Katmai Park and other regional wildlife refuges.

Van Hartley
4540 Edinburgh Drive
Anchorage, AK 99515
Telephone (907) 248-3539

P. O. Box 545
King Salmon, AK 99613
Telephone (907) 246-3437

Bristol Bay Air Service. To Dillingham area. Air taxi service. Unguided fly-out fishing.

John Bouker
P. O. Box 1135
Dillingham, AK 99576
Telephone (907) 842-2227

Era Aviation (and ***Alaska Airlines*** Commuter Service). Major regional airline. Destinations from Anchorage include towns of

Bethel, Homer,
Iliamna, Kenai,
Kodiak and Valdez.

Toll Free 1-800-
426-0333; Telephone
(907) 243-3300

Freshwater Adventures, Inc. To destinations in Dillingham area. Grumman Goose and Widgeon amphibian aircraft for fresh water charter. Raft rentals.

Phil Bingman
P. O. Box 190875
Anchorage, AK 99519
Telephone (907) 243-7676; Fax (907) 248-0021

Iliamna Air Taxi, Inc. To destinations in Iliamna area. Air taxi charter for fishing, backpacking, flight seeing, raft rental and lodging.

Tim and Nancy La Porte
P. O. Box 109
Iliamna, AK 99606
Telephone (907) 571-1248, Fax (907) 571-1244

Kachemak Air Service, Inc. To Homer for nearby parks including Brooks, Katmai and Lake Clark. Float plane.

Barbara de Creeft
P. O. Box 1769
Homer, AK 99603
Telephone (907) 235-8924

Katmailand, Inc. King Salmon to Katmai National Park and surrounding area.

4700 Aircraft Drive
Anchorage, AK 99502
Telephone (907) 243-5448; Fax (907) 243-0649

Lake Clark Air, Inc. To Lake Clark and Bristol Bay area. Air taxi service, air charters, lodging, flightseeing, fishing and recreation packages.

Glen R. Alsworth
Port Alsworth, AK 99653
Telephone (907) 781-2211; Fax (907) 781-2215

Mountain River Transporting. To destinations in Iliamna and Pike Lake area. Fishing, air taxi on floats.

Gene Smart
P. O. Box 6923
Nikiski, AK 99635
Telephone (907) 776-5678; fax (907) 776-5874

Naknek Aviation. To Naknek and King Salmon area. Guided and unguided fishing, camping, sightseeing.

J. C. Tudor
P. O. Box 261
Naknek, AK 99633
Telephone (907) 246-3385

Regal Air. To destinations from Lake Hood to Anchorage area. Fishing, flightseeing, charter. Floats, wheels and skis.

Craig or Sarah Elg
P. O. Box 190702
Anchorage, AK 99519-0702
Telephone (907) 243-8535

Tikchick Airventures. To destinations in Dillingham area. Charter air taxi. Unguided fly-outs and float trips. Equipment rental.

Rick and Denise Grant
P. O. Box 71
Dillingham, AK 99576
Telephone (907) 842-5841

Trail Ridge Air. To Iliamna area and Mulchatna Drainage. Remote cabins, unguided fishing, float trips, day fly-in guided fishing trips. Float planes.

Geoff Armstrong
P. O. Box 111377
Anchorage, AK 99511
Telephone (907) 248-0838; Fax (907) 248-2658

Tucker Aviation. To Dillingham area. Air taxi to all area villages.

Tom and Patty Tucker
P. O. Box 1109
Dillingham, AK 99576
Telephone (907) 842-1023; Fax (907) 842-2600

Uyak Air Service. To Kodiak Island area. Air charter on floats and wheels. Camping gear, boat, motor rentals. Sightseeing, fishing, float trips.

Oliver (Butch) Tovsen
P. O. Box 4188
Kodiak, AK 99615
Telephone (907) 486-3407; Fax (907) 486-2267

White's Air Service. To South Central Alaska (Anchorage area), on demand air taxi flight seeing and drop-off fishing.

Carl (Skip) White
P. O. Box 412
Kenai, AK 99611
Telephone (907) 283-4646

Pen Air. Regional airline. Destinations from Anchorage include towns of Aniak, Cold Bay, Dillingham, Dutch Harbor/Unalaska, King Salmon, Kodiak, St. George and St. Paul.

Toll Free 1-800-448-4226
Telephone (907) 243-2485
Fax (907) 243-6848

Yute Air Alaska. To Dillingham and Bethel area. Single engine and twin engine charter and scheduled service. Amphibious float planes to rivers, lakes and ocean bays.

Steve Huddleston
P. O. Box 890
Dillingham, AK 99576
Telephone (907) 842-5333

Ketchum Air Service (Day fishing)

Lake Hood, International Airport
1-800-433-9114, Fax (907) 243-5525

Rust Air Service (Day fishing)

Lake Hood, International Airport
1-800-544-2299, Fax (907) 248-0552

Rust's Flying Service (Guided and unguided air taxi)

Owner Todd Rust
P. O. Box 190325
Anchorage, AK 99519
(907) 243-1595, Fax (907) 248-0552

Appendix

4

SEVEN RECOMMENDED TRIPS —
FROM ALMOST NO COST TO LUXURY

There may be readers who would prefer not to go through the step-by-step process in this book to develop a customized plan for an enjoyable, affordable fishing trip to Alaska. So to satisfy those who want to go straight to some trip options, I have selected seven locations from my travels in Alaska that I believe will provide a very enjoyable fishing experience.

I have been to every one of these facilities in the last several years and, assuming they have not significantly changed policies or the fish have not completely changed their patterns, I believe everyone will find the following trips satisfactory. They range in prices and are typical in cost ranges for the quality of services provided.

One note of caution: I have personally visited the following facilities and my descriptions are from my notes, and some of the information about features at each location was obtained from sources believed to be accurate. Your actual experience may differ because conditions can vary, including changes in weather, shifts in fish migration and other unpredictable factors. Before committing to a trip, I recommend that you check the latest predicted fishing conditions with the management of the facility you are visiting.

If you are interested in one of these trips, see Appendix 2 for contacts, addresses and phone and fax listings.

Anchorage Area Rivers - A Lowest Cost Option

If you wish to fish at the lowest possible cost, in waters close to Anchorage, a fly fishing tour of local rivers less than one hour's drive from downtown Anchorage may be the answer. No guides are needed and the only other costs are for basic housing, food, car rental and a license. Anchorage has many accommodations to choose from, in all price ranges. And there is also a wide variety of restaurants and large food markets.

Be prepared, however, for large crowds of people during peak salmon runs. The proximity to Alaska's most populous city and the low-cost auto access make fishing near Anchorage popular not only with residents, but also with visitors who arrive in campers from the lower 48 states.

My trip recommendations are organized by species of fish:

For king salmon ranging between 12 and 40 pounds, during the popular king season in June, Ship Creek next to the railroad station and just three blocks from downtown hotels is a popular fishing location. Eagle River, just north of town is also excellent, but fishing is limited to Saturdays, Sundays and Mondays for 30 days starting on the Saturday before Labor Day. Note that these rules are subject to change and the Alaska Department of Fish and Game should be consulted for the latest rules.

Sockeye salmon run between 4 and 8 pounds. The best sockeye area is in the saltwater offshore, near the mouth of Six Mile Creek, on the Cook Inlet side of Elmendorf Air Force Base. Fishing is only allowed inside the mouth of the river, not upstream of the marker wire.

Silver salmon run between 8 and 15 pounds from mid-July to end of September with a peak in August. Excellent locations for silvers include Ship Creek below Chugach Dam, Campbell Creek in town between Dimond Boulevard upstream to the C Street bridge, and Bird Creek just south of town about 25 miles toward Kenai.

Pink salmon run between 2 to 4 pounds with the males showing a predominant hump on the back (males are called Humpies). Bird Creek is an excellent location for pinks between mid-July and early August during even years (1998, 2000, etc.).

There are no significant resident fish (rainbows, chars and

graylings) in the rivers near Anchorage, except for lakes where they are stocked.

In addition to fishing, an entertaining pastime is to view salmon during spawning runs. In late June to early August, the kings may be seen at Chugach power plant dam on Ship Creek and at the Elmendorf Hatchery. Good viewing is also found at Rabbit Creek along Potters Marsh boardwalk, Campbell Creek upstream of Lake Otis Parkway and in the south fork of the Eagle River between the falls and the confluence with the river.

You can see sockeyes at the north fork of Campbell Creek above the Bicentennial Park or during August at Willowaw Creek in Portage Valley. The trip to see the sockeyes is short and includes a nice viewing of Portage Glacier. Silvers are seen at Ship Creek, Potter Marsh and Campbell Creek from mid-August to early October.

For further information and free brochures and maps, stop in at, or write to, the Department of Fish and Game, 333 Raspberry Road, Anchorage, AK 99518-1599.

If sparse accommodations are acceptable, you can stay in Anchorage for $50 or less per night. You can purchase food inexpensively at local supermarkets. Be sure to arrange your car rental ahead of time and don't forget your fishing license. The cost of a fishing license was $30 in 1996 without a King Salmon stamp.

Angler's Alibi on the Alagnak

Are you seeking a location in front of one of the best holes on one of the 5 best salmon rivers in Alaska, all at an affordable price? Then Angler's Alibi Camp on the Alagnak River in Bristol Bay may be your answer.

Located about 30 minutes north of the town of King Salmon, this location features non-stop fishing action during several runs of salmon in the summer and a chance to try for huge fish. The owner - manager - head guide is Karl Storath who makes his winter home in New York. I have known Karl for several years and my last visit was in 1995 when huge salmon was the hot action in July.

The camp is small and is able to tailor to guests' special needs with a capacity of only 9 guests maximum in a setting with elevated view of the Alagnak. There are 3 guides including Karl. All guides are accomplished fly fishing experts, most provide fly fishing guiding and instruction year-around in the lower 48 states.

The camp facility is very user-friendly with large tents, almost full sized cabin-like, for living and sleeping. There is a huge tent that includes the kitchen and dining area with a fly-tying table in the corner. Sleeping units are comfortable stand-up tents that have 3 beds, propane heater, lights and screened door and windows. There is a shower - laundry bathhouse cabin and two outhouses. Bedding and towels are provided, as well as laundry service.

The food is very good and plentiful and a professional chef prepares steaks, chicken, ham, salmon, fresh salads, baked breads and freshly prepared desserts. Happy hour is on the patio with a view of the river - appetizers are served with complimentary soft drinks, while other drinks are BYOB. Fishing waters are so close to camp that lunches can be served in camp or at shore lunches on excursions away from camp. Special dietary needs can be accommodated with advanced notice since supplies are ordered and delivered frequently by air from the town of King Salmon and Anchorage. I once asked for a special entree of the jaws, collar and belly of freshly caught salmon served with soy sauce. The chef served it with pleasure - a photo of the meal is in my seminar.

An advantage of a small facility is to tailor the fishing to customers' desires. For example, when I was there, we fished for huge kings, averaging 30 or more pounds. Next we fly fished for big chum salmon. Then another day, we went a long way up river for sight fishing for rainbows and graylings. Then in mid-week, we took a fly-out on a floatplane into Katmai National Park for rainbow and char fly fishing on small streams. During that trip, encounters with bears are likely and a terrific photo opportunity.

In the non-guided hours, guests can fish the Alagnak River immediately in front of the lodge or tie flies taught by the guides or on your own using materials provided by Karl. Fish caught early in the week are cleaned, prepared, frozen and packed for shipment home as extra luggage on the same planes you take home.

When fishing for king salmon, Karl uses a special large lure that includes yarn and a special Styrofoam ball, about the size of a golf ball. The most effective technique is to drift fish with the boat using conventional gear and save your arms from wearing out when compared to fly casting all day with a heavy rod and sinking line. But you can also use your favorite salmon attractor flies and cast in tidal waters. Another favorite fly fish objective is to use the Fuchsia Bunny Fly and wade for large chum salmon. The best "Chum Holes" are only a few hundred yards from camp and they take flies like hooking on to the caboose of a runaway freight train. Sockeye runs are immense and can be seen going up river in front of the lodge - but sockeyes are elusive and a challenge to get them to take flies. Rainbows and arctic grayling can be taken on your favorite dry flies and nymphs while chars will readily take egg simulations during spawning runs.

Price for 1997 is $2875 for a full week which compares to other lodges on the same river that go for up to $4000. Air transportation to King Salmon is paid by the guest, while the camp provides a round-trip floatplane for the last leg to the camp.

Aniak River Lodge in Aniak

When was the last time you stepped out of the lodge, walked a few feet, cast a fly and within a few casts caught a 10 pound salmon - all at an affordable price? No, you are not dreaming and I recently did it on the third cast and my friend caught a salmon on his first cast after stepping out of the lodge minutes after he arrived on the first day. So when the fish are running, Aniak River Lodge in Aniak may be your answer.

In a remote corner of the Southwest region, west of Dillingham and north of Bethel lies the small town of Aniak, at the confluence of the Kuskokwim River and Aniak River.

The location features outstanding fishing for kings, sockeyes, silvers and rainbows. The Aniak River Lodge includes a homey atmosphere, a very personable manager - Lee Brooks, small town environment and access to a modern medical facility - a real getaway place for great fishing.

The lodge is new and is just getting started. Although a cabin was operating in 1996 with a staff of two, the plan is to complete the main lodge in 1997 and properly staff for a professional fishing lodge.

Therefore, the plan is to accommodate up to 10 guests with a staff of 4 guides, a professional cook and a manager.

Fly-outs will be offered as an option for upper river and lake fishing for large lake trout. Kings on Aniak run 35 to 65 pounds starting June 10 and ending about July 10. Sockeyes run 10 to 15 pounds starting July 10. Silvers run 8 pounds average and up to 12 or more pounds, starting at the end of July and running through all of September. Big rainbows exist, averaging 24 inches and a record of 34 inches was caught. Rainbows run all year, but the larger ones arrive mid August until end of September.

Fly fishing is readily accommodated, up to 100% of time, but ability to sight fish depends on rain and degree of silt in the water. The weather is unpredictable and opaque waters are possible at any time. Plans for fly fishing equipment rental, fly tying facilities and supplies were not yet set at time of this writing.

Buildings are relatively modern, including up-to-date flush toilets. A cabin houses a bedroom, small kitchen and toilet. The new lodge building is modern including showers and toilets shared by guests. Lounge and dining areas are planned to be on a common 2nd floor, but the lodge building was not yet finished in summer of 1996 to confirm the final configuration or furnishings.

Food is plentiful, but somewhat basic. The planned hiring of a professional chef should further improve quality of food. Custom and dietary meals are reported to be available on order. No alcohol is sold in Aniak - BYOB.

An anecdote - when my companion's airline lost his baggage in 1996, Lee Brooks stepped in and arranged a special flight to bring the lost bag, even when the airline was not scheduled to fly - a measure of Lee's professionalism at customer satisfaction.

The price for 1997 is $2100 for 7 days and 7 nights, not including round trip air from Anchorage to Aniak and return.

Camp Kiklukh, east of Cordova
Have you ever heard of dry fly fishing for salmon? Or wading as you sight fish to huge rising silver salmon? Well I never did until I heard about Camp Kiklukh, on the Alaska Gulf Coast east of Cordova.

The Kiklukh River, more accurately labeled a medium sized, moderately flowing stream, is located east of Cordova, a fishing village east of Anchorage and served by commercial airlines.

Camp Kiklukh was created when a land lease was secured from the State of Alaska in 1987. Then the owner, George Davis, created the first cabin in the summer of 1992, with the exclusive right to fish anywhere along the river from the ocean to its origin 30 miles upstream. The lodge is reached by taking a brief commercial flight from Anchorage to Cordova, then transferring to the lodge provided airplane, possibly George himself piloting his Cessna and landing at his private airfield carved out of the hard packed sand adjacent to the lodge.

This is a full service lodge consisting of a main cabin with kitchen and dining facilities, a separate cabin for recreation, two cabins for shower/washrooms, a sauna cabin, many cabins for guests housed two bunks to a cabin and four outhouses. Bedding is provided including comforters and fresh linens. The capacity is 16 guests supported by a staff of 7 including 4 guides - George Davis, George's two sons and Pat Pendergast, marketing manager. There are various boats and several ATV's - the main mode of land transportation. The recreation room includes a fly tying bench with supplies provided.

The primary feature is silver salmon fishing from mid-August until mid-October, during which time about 12,000 to 25,000 mature silvers arrive for their annual spawning run. These are not small silvers - by a quirk of nature, the average silver on the Kiklukh River is 12 pounds and occasionally run up to 20 or more pounds. The quantity of fish caught can also be impressive - the camp record is 257 silvers in one week. Also there are spring steelheads and sea-run dolly vardens. There are some rainbows in the medium size, but the primary feature is sight fishing to huge silvers in clear waters.

An exciting combination is to surf fish for congregating silvers at the mouth of the Kiklukh, just a half-mile downstream from camp, then follow waves of silvers coming in on high tide and attempt to have salmon take on surface flies. George developed a special wet fly, called the Davis Spanker which George or Pat can provide the detailed tying pattern if you plan to go to Kiklukh. Similarly, effective dry flies include the Pink Pollywog and the Dahlberg Slider (created by Larry Dahlberg of TV's "Hunt for Big Fish"). Several IFGA world records were set on this river - including a 22 pound silver salmon on a 12 pound test tippet and an 18 pound 7 ounce silver on a 6 pound test tippet. The certificate is proudly displayed in the dining room along with the mounted trophy.

The camp, more accurately called a lodge, is made of up multiple wood-sided cabins and wood fueled heaters in each cabin. There are many other activities available for those who wish a more total adventure visit to Alaska. There are several animals and birds, as well as a varied wild plant life on which George's wife, Debbie, is an expert. Wildlife includes bears, moose, wolves, beavers eagles and goats. For photo hobbyists or professionals, the surrounding spruce forested hills, logs brought in with the tide, snow capped mountains and huge glaciers are a sight to be seen and photographed. Taking an ATV trip with a camera to get glacier ice for coolers is a visit not to be missed.

One of the special features is Debbie Davis' cooking - typical meals include Filet Mignon with Prawns, Baked Fresh Halibut, Cornish Game Hen, Prime Rib with King Crab, Grilled Salmon and homemade baked desserts. Special diets are accommodated with advanced notice. Clean, cool water comes from a natural spring and happy hour features BYOB and the camp provides all setups. Pre dinner and post-dinner gatherings around the campfire is a memorable highlight.

Planned price for 1997 is $2700 including round trip air transportation from Cordova. Partial week stays can be arranged if space is available.

Great Alaska Fish Camp in Kenai Peninsula
Ten years ago, Great Alaska Fish Camp was the first lodge (yes it is better described as a lodge than a camp) that I went to in Alaska and my repeat trip in 1996 confirmed that the fishing action is as good as it was a decade ago. When in Anchorage with limited time, but you crave for a chance at huge salmon and large rainbows and wish to combine the trip with wilderness tours - without renting a vehicle or paying for local air taxis - Great Alaska Fish Camp may be for you.

The lodge was created by Kathy Pedersen's parents as home-steaders and built the lodge in the current premier location at the confluence of the Kenai and Moose rivers. It is on the highway to Homer, just before Soldotna on the Kenai Peninsula. The lodge provides free transportation from downtown Anchorage hotels and provides aircraft transportation back to Anchorage. The drive between Anchorage and Great Alaska is one of the most scenic on the Alaska highway system and includes stops at Portage Glacier and driving through several lakes and mountain forests.

This is a full service lodge with guiding provided every day. The head guide Russ is an excellent and patient guide, catering to both fly fishers and conventional gear fishers. The guests - to - guide ratio can be as high as 4 to 1 but the float trips are limited to 2 to 1. There are fly-out trips that place you in remote mountain streams with almost no others fishing in sight.

There are several animals that could be encountered including bears and moose. The best fishing is for kings (the Alaskan record of 97 pounds was set on the Kenai River), sockeyes, silvers and rainbows. At this location, fly fishing professional Jim Teeny set a daily record of 63 kings caught and released in one day.

The water is opaque and aquamarine like most glacial waters. Some first-time visitors are disappointed in not being able to sight fish in this famous river, but for very large fish, this lack of sight fishing is common in Alaskan waters that are glacially-fed. The weather is somewhat unpredictable, typical of most of Alaska. Be prepared by bringing good quality raingear. The best fishing for rainbows are done in the upper Kenai river, where float drifting is the only solution for covering large areas of the river. So under this situation, one gets out of the anchored boat and wades to desirable casting positions.

There are many people on the Kenai, especially during the summer salmon runs. As a result the camp awakens early, about 4:30 a.m., to get the guests to the premium fishing holes ahead of the crowd. Then the guiding stops at 3:00 p.m., early enough to return to the lodge, rest and fish again in front of the lodge as long as desired into the night. Sunset in July is near midnight and sunrise is near 5:00 a.m.

There are no fly tying facilities or supplies in the camp - if this is important to you, bring your own tying gear. On casting equipment, spinning rods and level wind gear are provided. Fly tying rods and reels are not stocked. Unlike most of remote Alaska, there are several fishing equipment stores are in the nearby towns of Kenai and Soldotna.

Housing is in multiple units arranged in bungalows on a bluff overlooking the Kenai and Moose Rivers. There is a flush toilet / shower within each unit. Also a central bathhouse and Jacuzzi is in the complex. There is adequate hot water and the electricity runs 24 hours a day.

The main building includes two lounges and a dining room. Chef Philip does an excellent job which can include Filet Mignon, Pork Loin, Halibut, Prawns, Scallops, and barbecues. There are cold and hot appetizers and a happy hour with house provided cocktails and dinner served with wine / beer.

The price per week for 1997 is $3195 and includes salmon fishing, one fly-out, a halibut trip, and Upper Kenai rainbow fishing.

There is a special guided, low-cost trip priced at nearly one-half of the cost of a full service trip. Please contact the lodge for further details.

Rainbow King Lodge at Iliamna

What is a recommendation for a luxury lodge doing in a book on affordable fly fishing? The same reason that Mercedes and Lexus cars are featured in Consumers Reports. Sometimes people can afford the finest quality products and services and want to be discriminating to find the best value for highest quality.

Rainbow King Lodge at Iliamna is just one of those places dedicated to the finest fresh water fishing in the world, and my experience indicates they are close to that claim. Located on Lake Iliamna, 3 miles from the town airport and the Newhalen River, this is an outstanding facility with finest quality fishing, high quality accommodations, gourmet food, personal dedication to highest quality services and a management committed to the finest in fly fishing.

The lodge was built in 1971 by Ray Loesche, originally as a big game hunting lodge. In 1989, Tom Robinson and a group of Oregon investors bought the lodge and made further improvements. They cater to the clients who are very demanding - corporate groups and individuals who want the best.

The lodge owns 4 high performance aircraft - Two deHavilland Otters and two Beavers. One of the Beavers has large wheels to allow landing on sandy beaches and other remote unimproved surfaces. Every day is planned using float planes and a wheeled plane to get to waters as far away as Kodiak Island or Dillingham or further for the best fishing regardless of a species arriving early or late. Daily fishing choices include all five species of salmon, trophy rainbow trout, grayling, arctic char, pike and ocean fishing for halibut.

A feature of the lodge is they have exclusive leases to fish key portions of 5 major rivers - Copper, Dream, Gibraltar, Newhalen Gorge and Southeast. Recently on the Copper River (the one in Southwest, not the one east of Anchorage), over 60 rainbows were caught in one day and 20 of the fish were over 26 inches long! The world record rainbow on a 6 pound tippet was caught here - weighing 14.5 pounds.

The building facilities are appropriate to a luxury lodge - several spacious buildings including a main building with large dining room and lounge room and a separate recreation / lounge building. Bedrooms are spacious, comfortable and include large storage and hanging spaces. Bathrooms are built-in for all bedrooms and modernly equipped.

Food is outstanding, gourmet meals cooked to order and hot appetizers on a cart are served in the recreation room. An example dinner includes Mango and Avocado salad with Radiccio and baby greens, Bourbon - Pecan encrusted Rack of Lamb with honey mustard cream sauce and country style redskin potatoes with roast garlic and asparagus tips.

Fly tying facilities and supplies are provided. Fly fishing equipment is also provided at no additional cost. Latest clothing for fishing is available for sale.

Flightseeing is available at no extra cost - a feature used by spouses and others who want a break from the daily fishing activities. Trips to see volcanoes, glaciers, wildlife, clam digging, bears and other features of Alaskan environment are available.

A minor irritant - the town of Iliamna is dry, no liquor is for sale. So almost everyone does BYOB or orders it shipped in as personal property from Anchorage suppliers.

Price in 1997 for one of the finest in the region - $4,950 per week complete and no tipping. For those who can afford it, a very special place, access to very productive, leased waters and luxury service and gourmet food at a reasonable price. Partial weeks are possible but must be booked late when there are possible openings.

Talaview Lodge - northwest of Anchorage

Where can you take a 35 minute ride by lodge-provided air taxi from Anchorage and be in a pristine, remote wilderness river ideal for wading and fly fishing with very few other fishing people in sight? The answer could be Talaview Lodge on the Talachulitna River.

This lodge was started in June of 1978 by Steve and Louise Johnson beginning with a single A-frame cabin. Since then, Steve designed and hand built all cabins including the impressive large main lodge out of hand-trimmed logs. The air taxi departs from Merrill Field, near downtown Anchorage and 20 minutes from the international airport.

The features of Talaview Lodge include outstanding scenery for photography, very good fly fishing for in-season salmon and rainbows, few people, no roads, easy wading through the entire river and spacious landscaped grounds.

Both Steve and Louise live on the property throughout the year - assuring the highest quality of facilities and staff during the fishing season. Louise runs the office and provides a warm greeting and interesting discussions during your stay while Steve manages and maintains the property. Ask Steve for an interesting dialogue on how the log cabins were built.

The capacity of Talaview is 14 guests with 7 guides - a good 2 to 1 ratio. There are no fly-outs but there is ample opportunity to walk to fish. Nature hikes are available. Boats are taken only downstream to deeper waters near the junction with the Skwentna River. From the lodge high on the hill, there are outstanding views for photography. Many animals include bears, moose and many birds.

The walk for large rainbows can be tiring if not in shape - walking on boulders up river for several miles can be difficult, especially when followed by the 140 steps up hill to the lodge. Solution is to take your time and pace yourself.

The best fishing is for kings from June 11 to July 4. Chums arrive from July 15. Silvers run from late July and run through 3rd week of August. Rainbows are available throughout the summer. For variety of fish species, the best week is the last week in July. Fishing equipment is available for rent. Many unique flies are designed and tied by Steve and are for sale in the small retail shop, including Stevie's Wonder - a very effective Elk Hair and Grizzly Hackle combination.

Two types of accommodations are available. The standard cabin has 4 bunks with separate bathhouse . The deluxe cabin is a comfortable room with built-in bathroom. Plenty of hot water and showers and flush toilets. Very good food including freshly-made desserts. Entrees include salmon, turkey, roast beef and pork loin.

Price is $2630 to $3050, depending on cabin style for 7 days / 6 nights, but partial week stays are common and can be arranged.

Appendix

5

PLACES TO STAY IN TOWNS AND CITIES

The following places to stay in towns and cities may be of help if you are arranging for do-it-yourself trips.

It is almost impossible to not stay in Anchorage overnight at the start of the trip. Most flights from the lower 48 states and overseas arrive in Anchorage in late afternoon or evening. Then the regional Alaskan flights takeoff the next day in the morning or mid-day to remote towns and rivers. Most of the luxury hotels or near-luxury hotels and inns charge a premium during the summer season when the market is willing to pay high prices. The solution is to search for alternatives that do not charge as much. The section below on places to stay in Anchorage includes many choices.

To save money in Anchorage, ask if the lodging provides transportation from and to the airport. Most of these facilities also have connections with local experienced guides, so you might inquire on referrals. The noted prices are listed prices as of 1996 and may be subject to adjustments. Some restaurants, such as the colorful Sourdough Mining Company, provide free shuttle service to and from the restaurant. Therefore, renting a car or hiring a taxi (both expensive in Anchorage) is not necessary if planned properly.

Lodging in Denali National Park is listed because many first timers to Alaska should see this immense attraction of Alaskan nature. It takes at least one night and a long day to see the minimum tour of this park and the towering Mt. McKinley (if not clouded over).

An interesting fishing excursion to add to a trip of flyfishing is to go for ocean halibut fishing. To catch a magnificent halibut weighting up to 200 pounds or more is a memorable experience. The flavor of fresh halibut is unforgettable and could spoil you into no longer ordering the frozen variety. To do an all-day halibut boat trip requires staying 2 nights in local lodging. Homer and Seward are the two towns where fishing boats make a home port. Homer has the advantage of being closer to the halibut region in the Cook Inlet, but it takes about 5 hours of driving from Anchorage. Seward is closer, about 3 hours drive, but it takes longer on the boat to get to the halibut, about 2 to 3 hours.

Lodging on Kodiak Island is listed because it is usually an all-day trip by car and ferry to get to the island from Anchorage. Once there, an auto is handy since several rivers are reachable by auto.

Valdez is an all-day drive from Anchorage with many sightseeing spots and streams for fishing along the way. Once in Valdez, one option is to go for local salmon fishing on a boat in Prince William Sound. Sightseeing boats to view glaciers are also based in Valdez.

Anchorage

8th Avenue Hotel - In downtown, 28 clean, quiet, spacious one and two bedroom suites, full kitchens. Nonsmoking rooms, cable TV, laundry, free parking. Pets with approval. Close to dining, shops, attractions. Rates $120 to $145 summer. Credit cards. P. O. Box 200089, Anchorage, AK 99520. Phone (800) 478-4837, Fax (907) 272-6308.

15 Chandeliers Bed and Breakfast - Elegant with private baths. Buffet breakfast choices. Smoking outside only. Freezer storage. DeArmoun Road, close to bike path, waterfowl nesting, Chugach Mountains. German also spoken. Rates $90 to $110 summer. P.O. Box 110827, Anchorage AK 99511. Phone / Fax (907) 345-4935.

A Arctic Loon Bed and Breakfast - Very nice home with view and Scandinavian style. Eight person hot tub, sauna, hiking, golf, quiet mountain setting. Full breakfast. Rates $85 - $105 summer. Credit cards. P. O. Box 110333, Anchorage, AK 99511. Phone / Fax (907) 345-4935.

A Blackberry Bed and Breakfast -In Anchorage's Sand Lake area. Close to airport, downtown, Seward Hwy, trails, shops, museums and other attractions. Deck with view, private baths, suite with sitting room, laundry. 6060 Blackberry St., Anchorage AK 99502. (907) 243-0265.

A Garden House Bed and Breakfast - Accommodations include suite, king bed, private bath, sauna, TV, phone. Guest room with queen bed., TV and shared bath. Full breakfast. Rates $65 to $95 year round. 1511 Woo Blvd., Anchorage, AK 99515. Phone / Fax (907) 344-3312.

A TO ZZZZ Bed and Breakfast - Quiet setting with 15 foot floor to ceiling windows and fireplace. Overlooks park reserve and nature walk. Mountain view. Deck with hot tub. Private baths with double room suite available. Freezer. Licensed. Smoke-free, near airport. Rates $60 to $90. 2701 W. 80th, Anchorage, AK 99502. Phone (907) 248-3436.

A View With A Room - Antique decor, spacious rooms, guest living room. Full breakfast. Near hiking trails with wildlife. Peaceful atmosphere, sunset view. Rates $55 to $75. 8601 Sultana Drive, Anchorage AK 99516. Phone (907) 345-2781.

Alaska Bubbling Brook Bed and Breakfast - Spanish / Italian / Norwegian spoken. Full breakfast. Children welcome. Smoke-free environment. Laundry. Rates $70-$150. (907) 696-4854, Fax (907) 694-5104.

Alaska Chalet Bed and Breakfast - Located in Eagle River, northern edge of Anchorage. Handy to Eagle River self-guided fishing. Quiet, comfortable suite. Private entrance, kitchen, private / shared bath, sitting room. Full breakfast. View of Chugach Mountains from deck. Rates $65 to $85. 11031 Gulkana Circle, Eagle River, AK 99577. Phone / Fax (907) 694-1528.

Alaska Cozy Comforts Bed and Breakfast - Long time Alaskans and hospitable. Views of city / Mt. McKinley (if not clouded over). Fifteen minutes to airport. Full breakfast. Airport / train pickup possible. Rates start at $65. 10661 Elies Drive, Anchorage, AK 99516-1136. Phone (907) 345-1957.

Alaska Rose Bed & Breakfast - Comfortable home in quiet cul-de-sac along greenbelt. Salmon spawning during season   Hearty breakfast, sitting room, TV, VCR, laundry. Ten minutes from downtown and airport. No smoking. Rates $60 to $75 summer.   4607 Campus Circle, Anchorage, AK   99507. Phone (907) 563-4605.

Alaskan Frontier Gardens Bed and Breakfast - Alaska hillside estate on peaceful scenic acres by Chugach State Park. Spacious suites with Jacuzzi, sauna, fireplace. Large breakfast. Very comfortable. Rates $85 to $175 summers. Credit cards. Wheelchair accessible. P. O. Box 241881, Anchorage, AK 99524-1881. Phone (907) 345-6556, Fax (907) 562-2923.

An English Country Bed and Breakfast - Very comfortable, country decor. Full breakfast, evening appetizer. Private bath with queen bed. Very clean, garden-like setting. Near airport. Rates $70 to $90 summer. 2911 Rocky Bay Circle, Anchorage, AK 99515. (907) 344-0646.

Anchor Arms Motel - Downtown, at 433 Eagle Street, easy access to all services. All two-room suites. Airport courtesy van. Free HBO. Discounts for seniors, military government and airlines. Rates from $69 summer. Credit cards. 520 E. 4th Avenue, Suite 202, Anchorage, AK 99501. Phone (907) 272-9619, Fax (907) 272-0614

Anchorage Bed & Breakfast - Located near Chugach Mountains and lake fishing. On Chester Creek greenbelt. Outdoor hot tub. Main thoroughfares, bus routes and shopping nearby. Freezer / bikes available. Rates $65 to $75 summer. 2200 Banbury Drive, Anchorage, AK 99504. Phone (907) 333-1425. Fax (907) 337-0248.

Anchorage Downtown Bed & Breakfast at "Raspberry Meadows" - Studio garden apartment with queen bed, futon, kitchenette, fireplace, library, private bath, TV, phone. Walking distance to coastal bike trail, Westchester Lagoon, all downtown shops and hotels. No smoking. Rates $65 to $109 summer. Credit cards. 1401 W. 13th Avenue, Anchorage, AK 99501. (907) 278-9275. Fax (907) 279-9282.

Anchorage Eagle Nest Hotel - Studios, one and two bedroom suites with kitchens, full size appliances and dishes. TV and Laundromat, five minutes from airport. Courtesy van. On city bus line. Rates $99 to $170 summer. 4110 Spenard Road, Anchorage, AK 99517. Phone (800) 848-7852, Fax (907) 248-9258.

Anchorage Foothills Bed & Breakfast - Country style, suite with queen, two singles, private bath, or single, shared bath. No smoking. Children OK. Rates $40 to $75 summer. 2940 Brookridge Circle, Anchorage, AK 99504. Phone (907) 333-7704.

Anchorage Hilton Hotel - Large, first class hotel in heart of downtown. Huge mounted polar bear and brown bear in lobby. Tall building with views, 600 rooms, 3 restaurants, pool and spa. Rates $220 to $280 summer. 500 West Third Avenue, Anchorage, AK 99501. Phone (800) 848-7852, Fax (907) 248-9258.

Anchorage Hotel - Restored historic hotel, in center of downtown Anchorage. Complimentary local calls, newspapers, continental breakfast. Credit cards. 330 E Street, Anchorage, AK 99501. Phone (800) 544-0988.

Anna's Bed & Breakfast - View of Chugach Mountains. Sourdough waffles, homemade muffins Close to Elmendorf, bus, shopping. Also speak German. 830 Jay Circle, Anchorage, AK 99504-1876. Phone / Fax (907) 338-5331.

Arctic Fox Bed & Breakfast Inn - Downtown Anchorage. Rooms with private baths and suites with view. Continental breakfast. Cable TV, laundry, covered parking and freezer. Rates to $85+ summer. Credit cards. 326 E. Second Court, Anchorage, AK 99501. Phone (907) 272-4818, Fax (907) 262-4819.

Arctic Lodge - Near airport, restaurants and shops. Twenty spacious one and two bedroom units with kitchens, cable, free local calls and laundry. Nonsmoking rooms. Rates $69 to $98 summer. 5308 Arctic Blvd., Anchorage, AK 99518. Phone  (907) 562-9544, Fax (907) 562-9555.

At Schnell's Bed & Breakfast - Quiet street. Sourdough pancakes and reindeer sausage. Afternoon teas. Airport 3 minutes. Minutes from restaurants, downtown, bus and biking trails. Bikes, laundry, freezer available. Rates - $95 summer. Credit cards. 6608 Chevigny, Anchorage, AK 99502. (907) 243-2074 or (800) 777-2074. Fax (907) 248-9940.

Aurora Winds Bed & Breakfast - Suites with private bath, TV, phones. Four fireplaces, Jacuzzis, kitchenette, theater room, pool table, gym, outdoor hot tub, gourmet meals. Rates $95 + summer. 7501 Upper O'Malley, Anchorage, AK 99516. (907) 346-2533, Fax (907) 346-3192.

Bed and Breakfast on "K" Street - Walk or bike to downtown or coastal trail. Private room or apartment. Inlet view, private entrance, kitchenettes. Groups welcome Smoke free, secure neighborhood. Credit cards. 1443 K Street, Anchorage, AK 99501. Phone / Fax (907) 279-1443.

Bed and Breakfast on the Park - Downtown location. Converted historic log cabin church. Privacy. Full breakfast. Rates $90 summer. Credit cards. 602 W. 10th Avenue, Anchorage, AK 99501-3426. Phone (907) 277-0878 or (800) 353-0878.

Best Western Barratt Inn - Close to airport, free airport shuttle, 100 nonsmoking rooms, cable TV, full service restaurant, lounge. Phone (800) 221-7550.

Big Bear Bed & Breakfast - Alaskan hospitality in large log home with antiques, art and collectibles. Guest sitting area, VCR, videos, wildberry. Near downtown. Rates $65 to $85. 3401 Richmond Avenue, Anchorage, AK 99508-1013. Phone (907) 277-8189. Fax (907) 274-5214.

Brandywine Bed & Breakfast - Set against greenbelt, five minutes from airport, lakes, restaurants, shops. Full breakfast. Freezer and laundry. Rates $70 to $90. Credit cards. 2921 Brandywine Ave., Anchorage, AK 99502. Phone / Fax (907) 243-0889.

Camai Bed and Breakfast - Private bath in each of two suites. Quiet Anchorage neighborhood with stream in backyard. Rates start at $75 summer. 3838 Westminster Way, Anchorage, AK 99508-4834. Wheelchair accessible. Phone (907) 333-2219 or (800) 659-8763.

Caribou Inn Bed and Breakfast - Center of downtown business district and walking distance to bike trails. Across from Hotel Captain Cook. Walk to downtown stores and sights. Rates $69 to $99 summer. Credit cards. 501 L Street, Anchorage, AK 99501. Phone (907) 272-0444. Fax (907) 274-4828.

Chickadee Bed and Breakfast - Near recreation, public transportation and airport. Private guest level with mini kitchen. Sitting room with TV/VCR, two rooms with queen beds / shared bath. One room upstairs shares bath with host. Families and small groups welcome. Rates $55 to $70. 961 Coral Lane, Anchorage, AK 99515. (907) 345-4164.

Chugiak Bed & Breakfast - Rustic log home in quiet setting, 30 minute drive from Anchorage. Overlooks Bear Mountain near Chugach State Park. Breakfast with Alaska wild berries. 22774 Needels Drive, Chugiak, AK 99567. Phone (907) 688-2295.

Claddagh Cottage Bed & Breakfast - Located 1.2 miles from International Airport. Easy access to Lake Hood and major highways. Private bath and phone in room. Common TV and reading area. Rates $100 summer. Credit cards. 2800 White Birch Lane, Anchorage, AK 99517-3268. Phone (907) 248-7104.

Copper Whale Inn - Country inn in the heart of downtown Anchorage. Overlooks ocean waterfront with view of Alaska Range mountains. Summer whale watch. Historic house. Rates $110 to $145 summer. Credit cards. 440 L Street, Anchorage, AK 99501. Phone (907) 258-7999. Fax (907) 258-6213.

Cusack's Ramada Inn - Located in heart of Anchorage, six floors, 150 rooms, complimentary airport shuttle, free coffee / makers, refrigerators, free local calls, parking. Rates $120 to $200 summer. Credit cards. 598 W. Northern Lights Blvd., Anchorage, AK 99503. Phone (800) 235-6546, Fax (907) 561-7817.

Days Inn - Downtown - One hundred thirty rooms located in downtown near shops. Non smoking rooms, cable TV, free parking, courtesy airport transportation. Credit cards. Rates $135 to $150 summer. Wheelchair accessible. 239 W. Fourth Avenue, Anchorage, AK 99501. Phone (800) 465-4329, Fax (907) 258-4733.

Deals Bed & Breakfast - Clean, comfortable, secure rooms. All rooms have private bath in the room. Minutes from downtown, airport or major thoroughfares. Rates $95 summer. Credit cards. 2910 W. 35th Avenue, Anchorage, AK 99517. (907) 248-0031. Fax (907) 243-7711.

Deveaux's Contemporary Bed and Breakfast - Comfortable, well decorated home, queen beds and private or shared baths. Mountain view, minutes from airports and other main attractions. Full breakfasts. Rates 75-$95. 4011 Iona Circle, Anchorage, AK 99507. (907) 349-8910.

Down Home Bed & Breakfast - Homemade breads and jams. Near airport, restaurants, bus. No smoking. Rates $65 summer. 4520 MacAlister Drive, Anchorage, AK 99515. Phone / Fax (907) 243-4443.

Executive Suite Hotel - Spacious, full-kitchen suites, nonsmoking and handicap rooms available. Complimentary continental breakfast. Courtesy shuttle to airport, Lake Hood and Lake Spenard. Laundry and freezer. Rates $125 to $259 summer. Credit cards. 4360 Spenard Road, Anchorage, AK 99517. Phone (800) 770-6366, Fax (907) 248-2161.

Fernbrook Bed & Breakfast - Long time Alaska resident offers accommodations in Chugach Foothills near Chugach State Park. Pet an Alaska sled dog. Sourdough pancakes for breakfast. No smoking Quiet setting. Rate to $80. 8120 Rabbit Creek Road, Anchorage, AK 99516. Phone (907) 345-1954.

Garden Beds - Convenient location, phone, TV, laundry, gardens. Private entrance. Fully stocked kitchens for no-host breakfasts. Smoking on porch. Rates $125. 3105 W. 29th Avenue, Anchorage, AK 99517. Phone / Fax (907) 243-8880.

Green Bough Bed & Breakfast - Anchorage's oldest bed and breakfast. Country atmosphere, freshly ironed sheets, in-room phone/TV, storage. King, full, twin beds. Continental breakfast. Midtown location. Rates $55 to $75. 3832 Young Street, Anchorage, AK 99508. Phone (907) 562-4636. Fax (907) 562-0445.

Herrington House - Downtown European style renovated home. Near Museum of History and Art, Old City Hall, shops and Visitor Center. Boutique rooms with private baths. Fireplace, TV, phone, daily maid service, continental breakfast. 702 Barrow Street, Anchorage, AK 99501. Phone (800) 764-7666.

Hillside Hosts - Privacy, family groups, very quiet on acre of land. Near hiking and skiing trails. Rate $75. 7745 Port Orford, Anchorage, AK 99516. Phone (907) 346-3096.

Holiday Inn Anchorage - Newly renovated rooms and lobby, indoor pool and sauna, restaurant, lounge and meeting facilities. Hourly airport shuttle. Walking distance to theaters, convention center, shops and business district. Two blocks from visitors center. Credit cards. Wheelchair accessible. 239 West 4th Ave., Anchorage, AK 99501. Phone (907) 279-8671, Fax (907) 258-4733.

Inlet Tower Suites - Quiet, downtown neighborhood location, Courtesy airport shuttle, free local calls and parking. All rooms have microwave, refrigerator, views. Full service restaurant and lounge. Walking distance to downtown. Wheelchair accessible. Rates $130 to $195 summer. Credit cards. 1200 L Street, Anchorage, AK 99501. Phone (800) 544-0786, Fax (907) 258-4914.

Lakeshore Motor Inn - Located minutes from airport and Lake Hood. New rooms, family units, kitchen suites. Courtesy shuttle to airport, refrigerators, cable TV, laundry, freezers, complimentary coffee, teas, snacks. Rates $95 to $149 summer. Credit cards. Wheelchair accessible. P. O. Box 92696, Anchorage, AK 99509. Phone (907) 248-3485.

Lynn's Pine Point Bed & Breakfast - Quiet lodging in cedar retreat near the Chugach Mountains. Full breakfast. Tour planning and referrals. Rates $75 to $90 summer. Credit cards. 3333 Creekside Drive, Anchorage, AK 99504. Phone (907) 333-2244. Fax (907) 333-1043.

Midtown Lodge - Clean, private rooms with telephone and color TV, continental breakfast. Located in mid-town business district. Nonsmoking rooms available. Rates to $85 summer. Wheelchair accessible. 604 W. 26th Avenue, Anchorage, AK 99503. Phone (907) 258-7778.

North Country Castle Bed & Breakfast - Sunny Victorian hillside home. Mountain and ocean views on quiet forested acreage. Minutes from downtown. Large breakfasts. Rates $85 to $125 summer. P. O. Box 111876, Anchorage, AK 99511. Phone (907) 345-7296.

Northwoods Guest House - Near airport in quiet wooded area next to park and bike path, Three bedroom suites with full kitchen bath, phone, cable TV and laundry. Good for families. Rates to $135 summer. Credit cards. 2300 W. Tudor Road, Anchorage, AK 99517. Phone (907) 243-3249, Fax (907) 248-4709.

Puffin Inn - Courtesy shuttle from airport and Lake Hood. Free coffee and muffins. Freezer. Rates $96 to $116 summer. Credit cards. Wheelchair accessible. 4400 Spenard Road, Anchorage, AK 99517. Phone (800) 478-3346. Fax (907) 248-6853.

Puffin Place - One-bedroom suite / studio with kitchen. Within walking distance of restaurants and shops. Courtesy airport shuttle. Rates $116 to $166 summer. Credit cards. 1058 W. 27th Ave., Anchorage, AK 99503 Phone (800) 717-5223.

Red Ram Motel - Newly remodeled, cable TV, specialty rooms with kitchen, Jacuzzi. Downtown location. Phone (800) 215-7265.

Regal Alaskan Hotel - Luxury hotel, located on Lake Spenard, 248 rooms, in-room refrigerators, hair dryers, coffee makers, Lakeside dining, patio, lounge, float plane dock. Complimentary airport shuttle. Health club. Wheelchair accessible. Rates to $260 summer. Credit cards. 4800 Spenard Road, Anchorage, AK 99517. Phone (800) 544-0553, Fax (907) 248-5923.

Sheraton Anchorage Hotel - Large, 375 room, cable TV, hair dryer, coffee maker, iron / board in room, Nonsmoking rooms. Restaurant, nightclub, Sunday brunch. Rates $185 to $255 summer. Credit cards. Wheelchair accessible. 401 E. 6th Ave., Anchorage, AK 99501. Phone (907) 276-8700, Fax (907) 276-7561.

Ship Creek Hotel - Downtown location, views overlooking waterfront and Ship Creek. One bedroom suites with full kitchen, phone, cable TV, two blocks to restaurants, shops, attractions, railroad depot. Rates $125 to $145 summer. 505 W. Second Ave., Anchorage, AK 99501. Phone (800) 844-0242.

Sixth and B Bed & Breakfast - Downtown location. Complimentary bicycles. Free phone, snacks and beverages. Cable TV, videos. Across from museum, eight blocks to train station. Rates $58 to $98 summer. Credit cards. 145 W. Sixth Avenue, Anchorage, AK 99501. Phone (907) 279-5293, Fax (907) 279-8338.

Snowline Bed & Breakfast - Quiet hillside area. View of Anchorage, Cook Inlet, Mt. McKinley (on cloudless days). Twenty minutes from airport or downtown. Rates $85 to $105. Credit Cards. 11101 Snowline Drive, Anchorage, AK 99516. Phone (907) 346-1631.

Snowshoe Inn - Quiet, no smoking atmosphere in heart of downtown. Easy walking to tourist attractions, shops, dining, Cook Inlet and Alaska Railroad. Rates $75 to $100. Credit cards. 826 K Street, Anchorage, AK 99501. Phone (907) 258-7669. Fax (907) 258-7463.

Southseas Bed and Breakfast - Located near airport, shopping center, restaurant, lounge and room service. Private bathroom in rooms, easy bus access and airport pickup. Rates $69 to $99 summer. Credit cards. 3001 Spenard Road, Anchorage, AK 99503. Phone (907) 561-3001, Fax (907) 561-9191.

Super 8 Motel - Anchorage - Free airport shuttle. Laundry, conference room, free coffee, local calls and cable TV. Nonsmoking rooms and suites available. VIP Club 10 percent discount, kids under 16 free. Close to restaurants. Credit cards. 3501 Minnesota Drive, Anchorage, AK 99503. Phone (800) 800-8000, Fax (907) 279-8194.

Susie's Lake View Bed & Breakfast - Quiet setting overlooking Campbell Lake, garden setting, large deck, hot tub 24-hours a day. Close to airport. Rates $85 summer. Credit cards. 9256 Campbell

Terrace Drive, Anchorage, AK 99515. Phone / Fax (907) 243-4624.

Susitna Place - Quiet downtown location in 4000 square foot home. Cook Inlet, Alaska and Aleutian ranges viewed from large decks. Short walk to city center, coastal trail, bus route. Breakfast. Rates $75 to $135 summer. Credit cards. 727 N Street, Anchorage, AK 99501. Phone (907) 274-3344, Fax (907) 272-4141.

The Eagle River Log House Bed & Breakfast - On Eagle River, north of Anchorage. 10925 Corrie Way, Eagle River, AK 99577. Phone (907) 694-9231.

The Hotel Captain Cook - Very large, multi-building luxury hotel close to waterfront, heart of downtown, walk to shops, attractions. Rates $195 to $295 summer. Credit cards. Wheelchair accessible. P. O. Box 102280, Anchorage, AK 99510. (800) 843-1950, Fax (907) 278-5366.

The Voyager Hotel - Thirty eight large suites with air conditioning, refrigerator, wet bar, coffee maker. Downtown, easy walk to convention center, restaurants, shops, entertainment, attractions. Rates to $159 summer. Credit cards. 501 K Street, Anchorage, AK 99501. Phone (800) 247-9070, Fax (907) 274-0333.

The Treehouse Bed & Breakfast - Quiet residential neighborhood, close to bus, views, shopping, hiking, dining, airport. Outdoor Jacuzzi. Full breakfast in summer. Cats on premises. Freezer. Rates $50 to $90 summer. Credit cards. 13,000 Admiralty Place, Anchorage, AK 99515 - 3726. Phone / Fax (907) 345-5421.

Twelfth and L Bed and Breakfast - Corner of 12th Avenue and L Street downtown. Four rooms, each with private bath and cable TV. Many amenities. Shuttle to train station. 1134 L Street, Anchorage, AK 99501. Phone (907) 276-1225, Fax (907) 276-1224.

Two Morrow's Place Bed & Breakfast - Downtown, quiet neighborhood. Carriage ride or walk to dinner. Large breakfast with scones. Queen/twin beds, private/shared baths. Rates start at $80 summer. Credit cards. 1320 O Street, Anchorage, AK 99501. Phone (907) 277-9939, Fax (907) 272-1899.

Valley of the Moon Bed & Breakfast - Walking distance to downtown, overlooking Valley of the Moon park and coastal trail. Bicycles provided. Spacious and comfortable. Contemporary Alaska art collection. Rates $80 to $90 summer. 1578 E Street, Anchorage, AK 99501.

Phone (907) 279-7755, Fax (907) 279-2903.

Walkabout Bed & Breakfast - Downtown convenience. Short walk from all major attractions. Special breakfasts. Accommodates small groups. Rates for double $75. Credit cards. 1610 E Street, Anchorage, AK 99501. Phone (907) 279-7808, Fax (907) 258-3657.

Westmark Anchorage - Downtown tower hotel with 198 rooms and suites, banquet facilities, room service, restaurant and lounge. Coffee shop. Free parking. Rates to $210 summer. Credit cards. Wheelchair accessible. 720 West Fifth Avenue, Anchorage, AK 99501. Phone (800) 544-0970, Fax (907) 276-3615.

Denali National Park

Alaska's Mt. McKinley Motor Lodge - Quality lodging in center of Denali Park activities. Quiet rooms, panoramic views, TV, individual coffee makers. Conveniently located near shops and restaurants. No railroad shuttle. Rates up to $129 summer. Credit cards. P. O. Box 77, Denali National Park, AK 99755. Phone / Fax (907) 683-2567.

Backwoods Lodge - New family size rooms, drive-up parking, queen beds, private bath, TV, phone, kitchenette. Cedar log-sided lodge, set away from crowds, McKinley view (when clear). Rates $90 to $120 summer. Credit cards. P. O. Box 32, Cantwell, AK 99729. Phone (800) 292-2232, Phone/Fax (907) 768-2232.

Crow's Nest Log Cabins at Denali - One mile north of park entrance. Log cabins with hotel conveniences. View, extensive decking, complimentary coffee, two outdoor tubs. Courtesy transportation. Bookings for all activities. Rates $134. Credit cards. P. O. Box 70, Denali National Park, AK 99755. Phone (907) 683-2723, Fax (907) 683-2323.

Denali Backcountry Lodge - Located deep within Denali National Park. Full service accommodations. One to four night all inclusive packages with transportation throughout park. Daily activities include guided hikes, wildlife viewing, bicycling, photography and natural history programs. Credit cards. Winter contact - P. O. Box 810, Girdwood, AK 99587. Phone (800) 841-0692. Summer contact - P. O. Box 189, Denali National Park, AK 99755. Phone (800) 841-0692.

Denali Bluffs Hotel - Denali Park's newest hotel, close to Park entrance. Over 100 rooms. Each room has two double beds, private bath. Tour desk, gift shop, laundry, shuttle service. Rates $90 to $`195. Credit cards. Wheelchair accessible. P. O. Box 72460, Fairbanks, AK 99707. Phone (907) 488-7000, Fax (907) 683-7500.

Denali Cabins - South side of park entrance. Private cabins with bath, hot tubs, conference facilities, courtesy transportation to park and activities. Scenic grounds, mountain views. Spacious cedar cabins and family suites. Winter contact - 200 W. 34th Avenue, #362, Anchorage, AK 99503. Phone (907) 258-0134. Summer contact - P. O. Box 229 (Mile 229 Parks Hwy.), Denali National Park, AK 99577. Phone (907) 683-2595.

Denali Grizzly Bear Cabins & Campgrounds - South entrance Denali Park, overlooking Nenana River. Modern and kitchen cabins, old-time Alaskan atmosphere, tent cabins, RV hookups, tent sites, showers, groceries, gifts, liquor, ice, propane. Rates $49 to $99. Credit cards. Winter contact - 910 Senate Loop, Anchorage, AK 99712. Phone (907) 457-2924. Summer contact - P. O. Box 7, Denali National Park, AK 99755. Phone (907) 683-2696.

Denali National Park Hotel - Hotel is center for visitor activities in the Park. Restaurants, lounge, gift shop. Wildlife and natural history bus tours, rafting and flightseeing. Rates $97 to $149. Credit cards. Wheelchair accessible. 241 W. Ship Creek Avenue, Anchorage, AK 99501. Phone (800) 276-7234. Fax (907) 258-3668.

Denali North Star Inn - Eleven miles from Denali National Park, at Mile 248.8 Parks Hwy. Tour reservations. Alaskan gifts, beauty/barber shop, restaurant, sauna, recreation and exercise areas. Wheelchair accessible. P. O. Box 240, Healy, AK 99743. Phone (800) 684-1560.

Denali Princess Lodge - Large hotel, 280 rooms and suites with phones, TV, free shuttle to rail depot and park activities. Conference facilities, spas, gift shop, dining room, lounge and cafe. Rates from $99 summer. Credit cards. Wheelchair accessible. P. O. Box 19575, Seattle, WA 98109-1575. Phone (800) 426-0500. Fax (206) 443-1979.

Denali Riverview Inn - Beautiful views of Denali Park and sounds of the Nenana River, 12 rooms. Closest lodging to park entrance. Private bathrooms, TV, activity booking and t-shirt shop. Rates to $129 summer. Credit cards. P. O. Box 49, Denali National Park, AK 99755. Phone (907) 683-2663, Fax (907) 683-2423.

Denali Suites - Two and three bedroom, kitchen, dining area, living room, phone, TV and VCR, laundry. Located at mile 248.8 Parks Highway, 15 minutes north of Denali National Park. P. O. Box 393, Healy AK 99743. Phone (907) 683-2848.

Kantishna Roadhouse - Guided hiking, wagon rides to Wonder Lake, gold panning, mountain biking, flightseeing, wildlife photography. Premier lodging - cabins with private bath, fine dining, saloon, library, gift shop. Rate $560 double occupancy, includes room, transportation, meals and activities. Credit cards. Winter contact - P. O. Box 81670, Fairbanks, AK 99708. Phone (800) 942-7420. Summer contact - P. O. Box 130, Denali National Park, AK 99755. Phone (800) 942-7420.

McKinley Chalet Resort - Features suites, restaurant, espresso, beer and wine bars, indoor pool, hot tub, sauna and Cabin Dinner Theater, wildlife and natural history bus tours, rafting. Rates $117 to $181. Credit cards. Wheelchair accessible. 241 W. Ship Creek Avenue, Anchorage, AK 99501. Phone (800) 276-7234.

McKinley Village Lodge - Fifty comfortable rooms on the Nenana River, private baths, dining room, lounge, quiet location. Wildlife and natural history bus tours, rafting, Alaska Cabin Nite Dinner Theater. Rates $88 to $134 summer. Credit cards. Wheelchair accessible. 241 W. Ship Creek Ave., Anchorage, AK 99501. Phone (800) 276-7234.

McKinley / Denali Private Cabins - Private cabins, some with private bath, some with central bath. Closest full-service facility to park entrance. Free shuttle to railroad depot, wildlife trips and raft tours. Rates $99 to $119 summer. Credit cards. P. O. Box 90, Denali National Park, AK 99755. Phone (907) 683-2258.

Motel Nord Haven - Built in 1994 to serve motorists. Secluded location. Two queen-size beds in every room. Rates to $103 summer. Credit cards. Wheelchair accessible. P. O. Box 458, Healy, AK 99743. Phone (907) 683-4500, Fax (907) 683-4503.

Stampede Lodge - Gateway to Denali National Park, newly remodeled historic hotel, private baths, phones, kitchenettes. Bushmaster Grill and coffee shop, shuttle service, tour desk, Rates $80 to $85 summer. Credit cards. Wheelchair accessible. P. O. Box 380, Healy AK 99743. Phone (800) 478-2370.

White Moose Lodge - Near Denali, new, quiet, comfortable and reasonably priced rooms. Private bath and view. Complimentary continental breakfast. Convenient to restaurants, groceries, Laundromat. Rates $65 to $85. Credit cards. P. O. Box 68, Healy, AK 99743. (800) 481-1232.

Homer

Alaska's Pioneer Inn - Downtown Inn offers rooms with private baths. Kitchens available. Spacious yard and walk to restaurants, museum, beach. Rates start at $69 summer. Credit cards. Rental cars available. P. O. Box 1430, Homer, AK 99603-1430. Phone (800) STAY-655.

Bay View Inn - Every room overlooks Kachemak Bay and Kenai Mountains. Clean rooms, nonsmoking,. Options - kitchenettes, fireplace suite, honeymoon cottage. Rates $79 to $133 summer. P. O. Box 804, Homer AK 99603. Phone (907) 235-8485, Fax (907) 235-8716.

Beach House Bed & Breakfast - Quiet location on beach, ocean & mountain view, near Homer Spit boat piers, full breakfast, suite, Jacuzzi, queen bed. Rates $55 to $90 summer. P. O. Box 2617, Homer, AK 99603. Phone (907) 235-5945.

Brass Ring Bed and Breakfast - Log home in heart of Homer or private cottage on hillside overlooking bay. Hot breakfast. Outdoor hot tub, laundry, freezer. P. O. Box 2090, Homer, AK 99603. Phone / Fax (907) 235-5450.

Brigitte's Bavarian Bed and Breakfast - Two cottages, view over Kachemak Bay and Kenai mountains. Alaska library, private bath, gardens, full breakfast, sourdough breads, blueberry waffles, homegrown eggs. Rates $95. P. O. Box 23391, Homer AK 99603. (907) 235-6620.

Driftwood Inn - On Bishop's Beach, view Kachemak Bay's mountains, glaciers. Historic downtown. TV, stone fireplace in lounge, laundry, fish cleaning facilities. Rates $70 to $128 summer. Credit cards. 135 W. Bunnell Ave., Homer, AK 99603. Phone (800) 478-8019.

Halcyon Heights Bed & Breakfast - B & B in home of long time residents located at 900 foot elevation overlooking Kachemak Bay and Kenai Mountain range. Suite with private bath. Rates $75 to $115 summer. Credit cards. P. O. Box 35522, Homer, AK 99603. Phone (907) 235-2148, Fax (07) 235-3773.

Homer Bed & Breakfast - Comfortable and convenient, large living space, each apartment has two bedrooms, fully equipped kitchen, full bath. View. P. O. Box 856, Homer AK 99603. Phone (907) 235-22176.

Land's End - At tip of the Homer Spit on Kachemak Bay. View scenery and wildlife . Lounge and deck. Adjacent RV park. Rates to $150 summer. 4786 Homer Spit Road, Homer, AK 99603. Phone (907) 235-0400, Fax (907) 235-0420.

Lily Pad Bed & Breakfast - Rates $65 to $75 summer. Credit cards. 3954 Bartlett, Homer, AK 99603. Phone / Fax (907) 235-6630.

Magic Canyon Ranch Bed & Breakfast - View of Kachemak Bay, glaciers, mountains. Quiet location, hot tub, hiking, near recreational facilities, four rooms furnished with antiques, artwork quilts. Rates $75-$90 summer. 40015 Waterman Road, Homer, AK 99603. (907) 235-6077.

Manley's Bed and Breakfast - House located on Beluga Lake, variety of waterfowl and float plane operation. Fruit growing greenhouse and gardens. Rates $95. P. O. Box 955, Homer, AK 99603. Phone (907) 235-6766, Fax (907) 235-2551.

Sundmark's Bed & Breakfast - View of Kachemak Bay, Apartment and cabin with kitchens.. Outdoor sauna. P. O. Box 375, Homer, AK 99603-0375. Phone (907) 235-5188, Fax (907) 235-6998.

Kodiak

A-Wintel's Bed and Breakfast - Convenient location, non-smoking rooms, Alaska books and videos, gift shop. Fishing. Rates $60-$70. P. O. Box 2812, Kodiak, AK 99615. Phone (907) 486-6935, Fax (907) 486-4339.

Buskin River Inn - Located on salmon fishing and hiking/biking areas. Fifty-one clean rooms. Whirlpool suites. Restaurant and lounge. Free courtesy van, washer/dryer, refrigerators, credit cards and non-smoking rooms. 1395 Airport Way, Kodiak, AK 99615. (800) 544-2202.

Inlet Bed & Breakfast - New facilities, airport and ferry pickup, close to town near float plane lake, non-smoking rooms. Rates $55. Credit cards. P. O. Box 703, Kodiak, AK 99615. Phone (907) 486-4004.

Kodiak Bed and Breakfast - Views of fishing fleet, walk to galleries, museum, Russian church and restaurants. Fishing nearby. Rates $50 single, $60 double. Credit cards. 308 Cope Street, Kodiak, AK 99615. Phone (907) 486-5367.

Westmark Kodiak - Located downtown, close to shops and attractions. Renovated 81 rooms, dining room, and lounge. Rates

$104 to $108. Credit cards. Wheelchair accessible. 2365 Rezanof West, Kodiak, AK 99615. Phone (800) 544-0970, Fax (907) 486-3430.

Seward

A Cabin On The Cliff - Unique cabin rental, perched on 300 foot cliff overlooking Seward boat harbor. Hot tub on deck. Barbecue, Fireplace. Rates to $399 summer. Credit cards. P. O. Box 670A, Seward, AK 99664. Phone (07) 224-2723, Fax (907) 224-3112.

Alaska's Stoney Creek Inn Bed & Breakfast - Country comfort in a spruce tree setting. Deluxe rooms, private baths, queen beds. Rates $50 to $85. Credit cards. P. O. Box 1352, Seward, AK 99664. Phone (907) 224-3940, Fax (907) 224-2683.

Alaska Treehouse Bed & Breakfast - Set in spruce with mountain views. Rooms accommodate singles to groups. Minutes from harbor, glacier, hiking. Sourdough breakfast, espresso. Rates $70 to $85 summer. Credit cards. P. O. Box 861, Seward, AK 99664. (907) 224-3867.

Bay Vista Bed and Breakfast - One of my favorites - quiet forested neighborhood, very clean, spacious rooms with spectacular view of Resurrection Bay / Mt. Marathon. Large sitting area, phone, TV / VCR, refrigerator, microwave. Walk to boats, train, bus / trolley. Fruits, cereals, fresh baked breakfast. (Tell Vera I said hello). Rates $75 to $95. P. O. Box 1232, Seward, AK 99664. Phone / Fax (907) 224-5880.

Camelot Cottages - Cabins in woodland setting. Cabins sleep two to four. Private baths and complete kitchens. Also chalet for groups - sleeps eight with private bath, full kitchen, TV. Hot tub, laundry. Rates $70 to $150. Phone (800) 739-3039.

Clock's Bed and Breakfast - Clean, comfortable rooms with full breakfast. On salmon stream with view of mountains. Quiet country setting. Rates $55 to $85 summer. P. O. Box 1382, Seward, AK 99664. (907) 224-3195.

Creekside Cabins Bed & Breakfast - Rustic, cozy cabins and tent sites on Clear Creek, surrounded by tall spruce. Share heated restrooms with showers. Sauna. Off country road leading to spectacular Exit Glacier. Rates 55 to $75. P. O. Box 1514, Seward, AK 99664. Phone (907) 224-3834.

Eagle Song Bed and Breakfast - Quiet, country setting. Mountain view, easy commute to Seward. Queen beds, adults, no alcohol. Smoking outside, telephones. Full or continental breakfast. Rates to $75 summer. Credit cards. P. O. Box 2231, Seward, AK 99664. Phone (907) 224-8755.

"The Farm" Bed and Breakfast - Newly remodeled farmhouse. Private decks and patios, barbecue, walk in surrounding grassy fields, 20 acres. Rates $65 to $95. Credit cards. P. O. Box 305, Seward, AK 99664. Phone (907) 224-5691.

Harborview Bed and Breakfast Inn - All 8 rooms are non-smoking, have private bath and entrance, cable TV, phone, on-site parking, short walk to tours, downtown, beach walking and train. Breakfast delivered to room. Rates $85 summer. P. O. Box 1305, Seward, AK 99664. Phone (907) 224-3217, Fax (907) 224-3218.

River Valley Cabins - Six new hand-crafted cabins, private bath, sitting room, phone, continental breakfast. Wilderness setting, bird watching, wildlife. Minutes from boat harbor, town and Exit Glacier. Also, large, two bedroom cabin with full kitchen. Rates $107 to $150 summer. HC 64, Box 3517, Seward, AK 99664. Phone (907) 224-5740, Fax (907) 224-2333.

Seward Waterfront Lodging - Overlooks Resurrection Bay, trail bike path, downtown. Comfortable, convenient Alaskan home. Tour boats and restaurants nearby. Minimum two-night stay. Rates $75 to $100 summer. Credit cards. P. O. Box 618, Seward, AK 99664. Phone (907) 224-5563, Fax (907) 224-2397.

Wildflower Bed and Breakfast - Country style home. Wooded area with view of mountains and glaciers. Three rooms with king, queen or twin beds. Private or shared bath. Living room with fire-place, TV and VCR. Hot breakfast. Rates $65 to $85. P. O. Box 1641, Seward, AK 99664. Phone (907) 224-5764.

Valdez

Alaska Flower Forget-Me-Not Bed & Breakfast - Luxurious room and view of mountains and glaciers. Walk to nearby ferry and downtown area. Rates $65 to $80. P. O. Box 1153, 606 S. Waterfall, Valdez, AK 99686. Phone (907) 835-2717.

Angie's Downhome Bed & Breakfast - New accommodations with country decor. Continental breakfast with fresh baked breads. Rates $50 to $75 summer. P. O. Box 1394, Valdez, AK 99686. Phone (907) 835-2832.

Downtown B&B Inn - Comfortable rooms with private or shared bath. Cable TV, laundry. Close to ferry, charters, shops and restaurants. Family discounts. Rates $65 to $100 summer. Credit cards. Wheelchair accessible. P. O. Box 184, Valdez, AK 99686. Phone (800) 478-2791.

Gussie's Lowe Street Inn - Clean, comfortable rooms, Complimentary breakfast. Easy walking to shops, restaurants and tourist facilities. Cable TV, private or shared bath. P. O. Box 64, Valdez, AK 99686. Phone (907) 835-4448.

Keystone Hotel - Downtown, walking distance to ferry terminal, shops and restaurants. Newly remodeled, 107 rooms with private baths, TV, phone, nonsmoking or smoking rooms, Wheelchair accessible, laundry, continental breakfast. P. O. Box 2253, Valdez, AK 99689. Phone (907) 835-3851.

Lake House Bed & Breakfast - Views of mountains, alpine lake and birdlife. Secluded, but ten minutes from center of Valdez. Spacious accommodations. Rates $75 to $95. P. O. Box 1499, Valdez, AK 99686. Phone (907) 835-4752, Fax (907) 835-2437.

Tiekel River Lodge - Located halfway between Glennallen and Valdez. Cafe, gas, gifts, lodging, RV park, campgrounds, hiking, skiing, biking. Mile 56 Richardson Highway, Valdez, Alaska 99686. Phone (907) 822-3259, Fax (907) 822-5595.

Totem Inn - Rooms include two queen beds, private bath and shower, TV and phone. Restaurant opens at 4:00 am. Dinners specialize in fresh local seafood. Lounge. P. O. Box 648, Valdez, AK 99686. Phone (907) 835-4443, Fax (907) 835-5751.

Valdez Village Inn - Convenient, 100 rooms with private baths and cable TV. Restaurant and saloon. Conference and meeting facilities. Espresso shop and health club with whirlpool and sauna. Rates $90 to $129 summer. Credit cards. Wheelchair accessible. P. O. Box 365, Valdez, AK 99686. Phone (907) 835-4445, Fax (907) 835-2437.

Westmark Valdez - Overlooks picturesque small boat harbor, 97 rooms. Restaurant and lounge. Cable TV, banquet facilities, glacier cruise departs from hotel daily. Operated by Holland America Westours. Rates $98 to $149 summer. Credit cards. Wheelchair accessible. 100 Fidalgo Drive, Valdez, AK 99686. Phone (800) 544-0970.

More books for your fishing friends?
Or gifts for anyone for any occasion?

Order Form

Please send the following books:

☐ **Sam Mihara's Fly Fishing Alaska– $19.95**

☐ **Sam Mihara's Fly Fishing New Zealand (planned for 1998) – $19.95**

☐ **Sam Mihara's Fly Fishing Argentina (planned for 1998)–$19.95**

I understand that I may return books for a full refund, less shipping cost - for any reason - for a 30-day limit from the time of purchase.

Quantity _____

Title_____

Name:_____

Address:_____

City: _____ State: _____ Zip: _____

Sales tax: Please add 7.75% for books shipped to California addresses. Shipping: Add $4.00 for first book and $2.00 for each additional book. Books will be shipped upon clearance of checks or money orders. Book prices are effective until December 31, 1998.

Send order and check to: Eskay Publishing
16821 Greenview Lane
Huntington Beach, CA 92649

Feedback

Your comments and suggestions are highly valued. To receive advanced information on seminars in your region or information on future editions of this book and similar new books, please fill out the following information:

	Very Satisfied	Satisfied	Neutral	Dissatisfied	Very Dissatisfied
Quality of Overall Book -	_____	_____	_____	_____	_____
Quality of Text -	_____	_____	_____	_____	_____
Amount of Information	_____	_____	_____	_____	_____
Usefulness of Information	_____	_____	_____	_____	_____
Quality of Photos -	_____	_____	_____	_____	_____

Overall Comments and Suggestions:

_____

_____

_____

Send to: *Eskay Publishing*
              16821 Greenview Lane
              Huntington Beach, CA 92649

Your Name:_____

Address: _____

City: _____ State: _____ Zip: _____